**JESSICA DIXON & ARLENE HOLMES-HENDERSON**

# CLASSICS IN ACTION

**IN ACTION** SERIES

A **WALKTHRUs**
PRODUCTION

FROM HODDER EDUCATION

The Publishers would like to thank the following for permission to reproduce copyright material.

**p92** summary of expectations about Latin syntax used with permission of Johns Hopkins University Press, from *Classical World*, D. D. Markus and D. P. Ross, 98(1) (2004); permission conveyed through Copyright Clearance Center, Inc.

Although every effort has been made to ensure that website addresses are correct at time of going to press, Hodder Education cannot be held responsible for the content of any website mentioned in this book. It is sometimes possible to find a relocated web page by typing in the address of the home page for a website in the URL window of your browser.

Hachette UK's policy is to use papers that are natural, renewable and recyclable products and made from wood grown in well-managed forests and other controlled sources. The logging and manufacturing processes are expected to conform to the environmental regulations of the country of origin.

To order, please visit www.johncatt.com or contact Customer Service at education@hachette.co.uk / +44 (0)1235 827827.

ISBN: 978 1 9152 6184 7

© Jessica Dixon and Arlene Holmes-Henderson 2024

First published in 2024 by
John Catt from Hodder Education,
An Hachette UK Company
15 Riduna Park, Station Road,
Melton, Woodbridge IP12 1QT
www.johncatt.com

The authorised representative in the EEA is Hachette Ireland, 8 Castlecourt Centre, Castleknock Road, Castleknock, Dublin 15, D15 YF6A, Ireland

All rights reserved. Apart from any use permitted under UK copyright law, no part of this publication may be reproduced or transmitted in any form or by any means, electronic or mechanical, including photocopying and recording, or held within any information storage and retrieval system, without permission in writing from the publisher or under licence from the Copyright Licensing Agency Limited. Further details of such licences (for reprographic reproduction) may be obtained from the Copyright Licensing Agency Limited, www.cla.co.uk

Cover illustration © Oliver Caviglioli

Typeset in the UK.

Printed in the UK.

A catalogue record for this title is available from the British Library.

# REVIEWS

Classics in action is a truly wonderful book. What I particularly love about it is the way in which it demolishes the myths around Latin and Greek being solely the entitlement of the privately educated or the 'gifted' pupils in maintained schools. It draws together plenty of research to show that the largest gains are made with pupils with the greatest barriers to learning. Having taught Latin at lunchtime I know this is the case. It is also excellent in showing how classical themes can be incorporated into other subjects. There are terrific case studies, dealing with controversial themes, including classical texts in English at KS3 and clever ways of incorporating the subject at KS3. It is an absolute delight.

**Mary Myatt,** *education writer and speaker*

Whether you're new to teaching Classics or an established classroom practitioner, this is an indispensable guide to the teaching of classical subjects today. It gives a real sense of the vitality of a discipline that is constantly innovating, combining a rich and insightful picture of the Classics teaching landscape with bite-sized pedagogical wisdom drawn from across the subject community. The real beauty of the book and its practical application come from its respect for the enormously varied range of contexts in which classical subjects are taught and the pressures that teachers are under.

**Professor Sharon Marshall,** *University of Exeter.*

A comprehensive and valuable resource for all teachers of the ancient world.

**Steven Hunt,** *Associate Teaching Professor in Classics, University of Cambridge*

The authors provide a variety of functional and targeted methods to support PGCE students, ECTs as well as experienced teachers. The book provides an unparalleled insight into classical education in English classrooms.

**Lucie Kingscott-Marsh,** *teacher of Classics*

I regularly make reference to the John Catt *In Action* series as AHT Staff Development at a large north London academy; as an ex head of Classics I am delighted at the inclusion of this valuable resource for teachers (from novice to expert) of the subject. Despite the lack of much formal research into the current teaching of Classics in the UK highlighted in chapter 1, over five chapters, Jess and Arlene draw upon an impressive range of diverse and accessible case studies and resources. The 'hinterland of Classics teaching' in chapter 2 includes a particularly welcome reference to trauma-informed teaching of Latin stories, while chapters 3 and 4 deftly summarise key aspects of classroom pedagogy before modelling how each might be delivered in the Classics classroom. As expected from this series, the content and layout of each page make it quick and easy to draw upon one or two ideas for your next lesson. However, the book also provides broader frameworks and practical support for developing current schemes of learning or any new ones you might now be inspired to create.

**Julie Wilkinson,** *Harrow Collegiate Alliance*

*Classics in Action* provides a toolkit for Classics teachers to develop their practice. It will be valuable to all teachers of classical subjects, throughout their career, because of its thoughtful and actionable advice.

**Ashley Clinch,** *teacher of Classics, Thomas Gainsborough School*

# CONTENTS

|  |  |  |
|---|---|---|
| | Series foreword by Tom Sherrington | 6 |
| | Introduction | 10 |
| **Chapter 1** | What is Classics teaching all about? | 13 |
| | What do we mean by Classics teaching? | 13 |
| | What are the big ideas in Classics teaching? | 16 |
| | What can research tell us about Classics teaching? | 19 |
| **Chapter 2** | What does Classics teaching look like? | 23 |
| | What is at the core and in the hinterland of Classics teaching? | 23 |
| | What different forms can KS3 Classics curricula take? | 31 |
| **Chapter 3** | How can instructional teaching be used in Classics? | 44 |
| | What is Mode A and Mode B teaching? | 44 |
| | What does Mode A look like in Classics teaching? | 44 |
| | What does Mode B look like in Classics teaching? | 78 |
| **Chapter 4** | How can I develop reading, writing and speaking skills in Classics? | 86 |
| | Reading | 86 |
| | Writing | 101 |
| | Speaking | 116 |
| **Chapter 5** | Where can I go for further help and resources? | 118 |
| | Literature | 118 |
| | Resources | 119 |
| | Organisations | 120 |
| | Bibliography | 122 |

# SERIES FOREWORD

This series of books was commissioned as a WalkThrus Production to complement two of our other series: the *Teaching Walkthrus*, Volumes 1, 2 and 3, and the *In Action* series. We believe that, together, they represent a powerful resource for teachers in schools and colleges in multiple subject settings.

The *In Action* series has proven to be very popular with busy teachers, enabling them to engage with a range of important ideas from cognitive science and from education research more generally. In each book, the authors explore the key ideas from a specific researcher, translating them into practical approaches that teachers can adopt in their practice. So far, the series includes:

- Rosenshine's Principles of Instruction
- Collins et al.'s Cognitive Apprenticeship
- Fiorella and Mayer's Generative Learning
- Shimamura's MARGE Model of Learning
- Sweller's Cognitive Load Theory
- Wiliam and Leahy's Five Formative Assessment Strategies
- Annie Murphy Paul's The Extended Mind
- Dunlosky's Strengthening the Student Toolbox
- Berger's An Ethic of Excellence
- Bjork and Bjork's Desirable Difficulties
- Ausubel's Meaningful Learning

Each of these books is a guide to interpreting the research in ways that can be applied in real-world classrooms. We have been delighted by the response to the series, with teachers telling us they value the brevity and clarity and the examples of theory in practice. It's so important for teachers to have a good grounding in cognitive science so that they have not only a clear model of how learning happens but also an understanding of all the potential barriers or difficulties that students experience. Bridging the gap between research and practice is a significant challenge because real-world classrooms are so much more complicated than the controlled conditions usually set up to investigate specific concepts in trials. The authors of the *In Action* books are all serving teachers or have taught in schools for many years, so their take on the theories and concepts that their books focus on is important and incredibly useful, grounded in the reality of teaching whole, complex classes.

It's by no means a comprehensive list – not yet – and we recognise that many other aspects of research would benefit from the same treatment. Books on Nuthall's Hidden Lives of Learners, Engelmann's ideas on direct instruction and Bandura's ideas on self-efficacy are all in the pipeline. We would also encourage every teacher to engage with Dan Willingham's *Why Don't Students Like School?*

Released in parallel with the research-informed *In Action* series, our *Teaching WalkThrus* have also been popular with over 350,000 copies distributed across the three volumes. The idea of breaking ideas down into five-step visual guides, with short punchy descriptions, has proven very successful, allowing teachers to engage with a broad range of ideas in a very accessible format that informs their training, coaching or personal reflection. Significantly, *Teaching WalkThrus* were written in a style that is context free. They are generic in style so that teachers of all subjects in any setting can engage with them, transposing the ideas into their real-world contexts. The 150+ WalkThrus are organised into six main series, each of which represents an important area for professional learning:

## Behaviour and relationships
- Lesson management
- Planning for good behaviour
- Positive correction
- Relationships and mindsets

## Curriculum planning
- Assessment issues
- Broad design concepts
- Challenge, inclusion, diversity
- Detailed planning

## Explaining and modelling
- Giving explanations and modelling
- Reading and writing
- Standards, expectations and scaffolding
- Types of explanations

Questioning and feedback
- Assessment
- Core questioning techniques
- Deeper questioning techniques
- Feedback

Practice and retrieval
- Guided to independent practice
- Reading
- Building fluency
- Retrieval practice
- Support and challenge

Mode B teaching
- Choices and creativity
- Making it real
- Oracy
- Student-directed activities

With over 4000 schools having engaged with our online WalkThrus toolkit, we know that a great deal of valuable professional learning can be supported with our generic guides as a starting point. However, throughout each book we are at pains to stress the crucial need to adapt the ideas for specific circumstances. A five-step visual WalkThrus guide is not a set of rigid rules – it is a framework for thinking through an idea, deconstructing it so that teachers can then reconstruct it themselves, forming their own mental models for enacting powerful techniques in their own classrooms. That's the spirit.

Now, having explored research ideas in the *In Action* series and general pedagogical ideas in WalkThrus, we felt that the logical next step was to bring in subject-specific books in this new series, completing the third pillar of the trio: research, pedagogy, curriculum. Each book in the *In Action* subject series has been written by practising teachers who were tasked with presenting a summary of important ideas and debates from their subject to support busy teachers in their work. We have not imposed a rigid common format and our authors were encouraged to share their own perspectives with our readers. There is no definitive book on teaching science or history or maths or physical education – so these books are explicitly written with that in mind. The books represent the authors' personal perspective on how the ideas that circulate within each subject community can translate into great practice in the classroom. Once again, we invite readers to then adapt and adopt the ideas that make sense in their context.

I have to congratulate each author on their excellent work. It's daunting to summarise and capture the spirit of a subject, balancing depth of detail with sufficient breadth of coverage of content and related debates and implementation issues – all in what is meant to be a short book. If there is one thing that characterises all our books it is that they are accessible to teachers who are time poor. Each book in this series achieves that goal – they have an energy to them and a brilliant balance of rigour, steeped in experience with teaching the subject, alongside tons of examples to bring things to life.

We hope you find this book interesting and useful, adding an important dimension to your wider reading as a teacher doing the most important work there is: developing young people so that they have the knowledge, experience, confidence and wisdom they need to make sense of their world and play their part in the communities they belong to.

# INTRODUCTION

## What is the purpose of this book?

This book is for all teachers who are currently teaching, training to teach or interested in teaching classical subjects in secondary schools. It provides an introduction to the Classics education landscape for readers who are not yet familiar with the realities of teaching classical subjects in schools. For readers who are already teaching Classics or allied disciplines, we hope that the examples we showcase provide new ideas to enrich, enliven and extend your professional practice.

We have written the book in sections so that busy teachers can access its contents without having to start at the beginning and read to the end. We have included a range of QR codes, weblinks and references to promote further engagement with the ideas we sketch here. A list of the links to the QR code resources is given here:

www.hoddereducation.com/john-catt-extras

The book benefits from the input of practising teachers at various career stages. Some have university degrees and teacher training qualifications in Classics and Ancient History, others do not. All have extensive experience of teaching classical subjects successfully in secondary schools. We are very grateful to them for sharing their expertise with us and hope that their ideas spark further pedagogical innovation across the Classics teaching community.

The example exercises provided are based on the authors' own teaching practice. Many have been adapted from resources shared directly by other teachers or from our research into teaching and learning. We have provided references and links to the pedagogical principles that underline the approaches taken. Owing to the limited research into Classics pedagogy (which we address in chapter 1), much of this research has been into other subject areas and domains. As with all educational research, we advise individual teachers to find what works best in their setting, as classrooms are messy and complex educational contexts (Burnett and Coldwell, 2021).

Where possible, reference has been made to the original source material for resources. However, it is not possible to remember where every task, activity and format used in our teaching practice has been developed from and so doubtless some acknowledgements have been missed. We thank all who have shared their experience of best practice over the years and whose work has influenced our own teaching practice.

Some decisions were made for us. The dating convention BC/AD has been used here for two reasons. First, this is the house style of the publisher and is used in their History volume in this series. Second, the OCR exam board uses BC/AD in the current specifications. We would prefer, in future publications, to use BCE/CE, as per the American Historical Association.

# About the authors

**Dr Jessica Dixon**

Jess is Head of Classics at Woldingham School and for over a decade has taught all four classical subjects in the state and private sectors. Before this, she taught undergraduate seminars in Latin and Roman history while completing her PhD at the University of Manchester. She is the Latin representative for the Classical Association Teaching Board (CATB) and treasurer of the Association for Latin Teaching (ARLT). Jess has developed her passion for teaching and pedagogical research through the MSc in Learning and Teaching at the University of Oxford. She has also been inspired by the innovative craft shared by colleagues who generously contributed case studies.

**Professor Arlene Holmes-Henderson MBE**

Arlene is Professor of Classics Education and Public Policy at Durham University. She is the Director of the Centre for Classics Education Research and EngagementS (CERES) and leads the PGCE in Latin with Classics in Durham University's School of Education. A former Classics teacher in Scotland and England for more than a decade, Arlene is delighted to share her experience with those who are new to teaching classical subjects. She is Chair of the Department for Education's Expert Panel on Latin and advises several international organisations on curriculum, pedagogy and assessment in Classics. Among the volumes Arlene has edited are *Forward with Classics* (2018) and *Expanding Classics* (2023).

# CHAPTER 1
# WHAT IS CLASSICS TEACHING ALL ABOUT?

## What do we mean by Classics teaching?

'Classics' refers to the study of the languages, literatures, material culture and history of the societies of the ancient world, together with their influence on later periods and cultures right up to the present day. It is one of the most varied and interdisciplinary of all subjects and can include languages, literature, history, philosophy, art and archaeology. Within the English school curriculum, the word 'Classics' is often used as an umbrella term that can refer to any one of four examined subjects, available at GCSE and A-level:

- **Latin** is the study of the language of the ancient Romans. By GCSE level (offered by Eduqas and OCR), students read original Latin literature by authors such as Virgil, Caesar or Catullus. Although this course focuses primarily on language and literature training, there are opportunities to study the social and historical contexts in which texts were written.

- **Classical Greek*** is the study of the ancient Greek language. By GCSE level, students read original Greek literature by authors such as Homer, Thucydides or Euripides. There are opportunities to study culture and history, but, as with Latin, the focus of this subject is primarily linguistic. Although studying ancient Greek may help students learn modern Greek in the future, there are substantial differences between the two forms of the language.

- **Classical Civilisation*** involves the study of the literature, visual or material culture and thought of the classical world. There is no requirement to learn ancient languages. Topics for study at GCSE or A-level include diverse options such as 'Life in the Mycenaean age', 'Myth and Religion', 'The World of the Hero' and 'The Invention of the Barbarian'.

- **Ancient History*** enables students to gain a greater understanding of the ancient world and how its legacy affects today's society. Again, no learning of ancient languages is required. Although there is some overlap between the topics covered in Classical Civilisation and

Ancient History, the latter focuses more on military, political and social history, as opposed to literature and art.

* All GCSE and A-level qualifications in Classical Greek, Classical Civilisation and Ancient History are offered by a single examination provider, OCR.

In Scotland, qualifications are available in Classical Studies (at National 4, National 5, Higher and Advanced Higher) and in Latin (at the same levels).

The International Baccalaureate provides examinations in Latin and Ancient Greek at Standard and Higher Level. The IB also offers a Standard Level course in Classical Greek and Roman Studies.

Cambridge International offers an IGCSE in Latin and International AS and A-levels in Classical Studies.

## Classics in the curriculum

### England

In England, the study of the Greeks and Romans is a compulsory element of the Key Stage 2 (KS2) History national curriculum for young people aged 6–11. Teachers and learners in primary schools often reflect with fondness on the stories of gods, goddesses and gladiators that stimulate comparison and contrast to contemporary society.

Since 2014, Latin and Ancient Greek have been included in the KS2 Languages curriculum. This allows school leaders and primary teachers to teach an ancient language instead of, or in addition to, a modern language for young people aged 6–11. Holmes-Henderson has conducted research into the impact of learning Latin and Greek on children's cognitive development (2023a). These studies have shown that learning Latin offers particular benefits to students who speak English as an additional language, who have special educational needs and disabilities and who qualify for free school meals.

With funding available from Classics charities (see 'Organisations', p. 120) to train teachers, buy resources and co-finance educational visits linked to learning Latin and Greek, hundreds of primary schools have introduced an ancient language to their curriculum in the last decade (Holmes-Henderson and Kelly, 2022). Latin is now the fourth most taught language in primary schools in England (Woolcock, 2023, 2024).

Policy support for Classics disappears at Key Stage 3 (KS3). No classical subject appears on the national curriculum for 12–14-year-olds. At Key Stage 4 (KS4), policy support via the English Baccalaureate (EBacc) extends to Latin, Greek and Ancient History. These all 'count' as EBacc subjects. The treatment of Classical Civilisation as the 'ugly sister' in this regard is puzzling.

## Scotland

Scotland has committed to the EU's 1+2 Languages policy, guaranteeing that all children in Scottish primary schools will learn English or Gaelic plus two additional languages before they begin secondary education. Under this policy framework, Latin counts as an option for the third language and is currently taught in schools across several Scottish local authorities.

Scotland's Curriculum for Excellence awards parity of esteem to classical and modern languages. Classical languages have their own set of experiences and outcomes relating to:

1. translating texts
2. interpretation of texts
3. using knowledge about language
4. culture and heritage.

Classical Studies is included in the social subjects curricular area alongside Geography, History, Modern Studies, and Religious, Moral and Philosophical Studies. Classical Studies contributes particularly to the 'People, past events and societies' section of the curriculum.

## Northern Ireland

Classics is not compulsory in the Northern Ireland Curriculum (NIC) (CCEA, 2007). However, it is taught in a minority of Northern Irish post-primary schools, predominantly in the grammar sector. The *Language Trends Northern Ireland* Report in 2019 (British Council Northern Ireland 2019) showed that below 10% of post-primary schools had Latin timetabled; less than 5% had it as an extracurricular option. A more recent *Language Trends Northern Ireland* Report (British Council Northern Ireland, 2021) showed that 0% of surveyed schools had Latin as an option for students in Year 8. Only 1% had the option in Year 9. For further information on the benefits and challenges of implementing Classics as part of the NIC, see Taylor et al. (2023).

15

### Wales

The Curriculum for Wales (Welsh Government, 2023) represents exciting opportunities for the expansion of ancient languages. The Languages, Literacy and Communication Area of Learning and Experience addresses fundamental aspects of human communication. It aims to support learning across the whole curriculum and to enable learners to gain knowledge and skills in Welsh, English and international languages, as well as in literature.

Developing effective communication and literacy skills, as well as learning about etymology within this area, is prioritised to give learners better access to information, concepts and terminology. The role for Greek and Latin in boosting etymological awareness is expansive.

Classical Civilisation and Ancient History contribute directly to the Humanities Learning area. The study of literature plays a vital role in shaping and influencing the development of communities and societies. Literature provides valuable evidence for, and can be a focus of, enquiries in Humanities. Learners can explore literature from a range of cultures and societies, in the past and present, from their locality, Wales and the world.

## What are the big ideas in Classics teaching?

### Pedagogical approaches

Latin and Greek

A number of pedagogical approaches are used in schools to teach Latin and Greek. Some teachers and researchers advocate strongly for one particular approach, but others find that their teaching practice is a blend of elements from two or more.

- **Grammar–translation** – this traditional approach to language learning prioritises the learning of accidence, grammar and vocabulary to help students move quickly from word level to sentence level to passages. It is characterised by rote-learning tables and charts of noun and verb endings, often 'chanted' aloud as a choral activity in class. The focus is on reading and writing, with little (or no) attention paid to using Latin or Greek as languages to communicate orally.

- **Reading approaches** – exemplified by courses such as *Ecce Romani*, the *Cambridge Latin Course* and *Suburani*, the reading method uses an ongoing storyline specially written to teach linguistic and cultural material. Accidence, grammar and vocabulary are introduced in carefully scaffolded ways, alongside memorable characters, locations and events, to boost learner engagement and encourage continuation.

- **Communicative approaches** (e.g. Living Latin/Greek) – these are popular in the USA and teach Latin and Greek as modern languages. Students listen to ancient languages being spoken by teachers and are encouraged by specially designed textbooks to engage in conversation to improve their language learning. In classrooms where communicative approaches are used, teachers and students report improved reading comprehension. A high level of language competence is required to teach ancient languages communicatively. Summer schools and training courses exist to help teachers up-skill in this area.

### Classical Civilisation and Ancient History

The volume of material available for study of Classical Civilisation and Ancient History means that, at KS3, it is necessary to identify ways to focus on topics or themes. Enquiries – built on the basis of genuine, worthwhile historical questions that students are ultimately required to answer – often form the basic units within schemes of work, with each enquiry lasting several lessons or weeks. A good question will make clear not only the substantive focus of the enquiry but also the particular second-order or disciplinary concept that students are dealing with. Enquiry questions (EQ) are popular in the history teaching community (Olivey, 2022).

Examples include:

- What can the Olympic Games tell us about the ancient Greeks?
- What impact did the Romans have on Britain?

This approach allows teachers to plan effectively across key stages, clearly identifying where and when they are focusing on particular concepts, making it easier to plan for progression. For exemplification of how this works in Ancient History at KS3–KS4, see McOmish (2023) and her case study (pp. 37–40) on integrating Ancient History into the KS3 History curriculum.

## Debates and dilemmas in the subject community

For a small subject community, there are plenty of areas of disagreement. We outline four here.

17

### Languages versus the study of antiquity in translation

There exists some intellectual snobbery around the study of ancient languages, with some Classics teachers, school leaders and academics believing that Latin and Greek are superior subjects, and of greater academic value, than Classical Civilisation and Ancient History. There is no substance to this invective. If anything, research by Hunt and Holmes-Henderson (2021) revealed that the relative difficulty of Classical Civilisation and Ancient History is greater than that of ancient languages.

Classical Civilisation has been described by classicists as 'intellectual baby food' and the 'diet coke of Classics' (Holmes-Henderson and Hall, forthcoming). These slurs may indeed be responsible for the exclusion of Classical Civilisation from the EBacc. The authors encourage readers to view all classical subjects as equal in the qualification ecosystem.

### Classics: for the many or the few?

Controversy surrounds access to classical subjects in schools. Data showcasing the types and locations of schools teaching Classics can be found in Hunt and Holmes-Henderson (2021). It will come as little surprise that Latin and Greek are predominantly available in the fee-paying sector and are more commonly available in London and the South of England.

But in schools that offer classical subjects, who is allowed to learn them? This might appear an unusual and shocking question to subject specialists in Maths, for example. Surely everyone is allowed to learn a subject on the curriculum? It has historically been the case that some schools limit access to Latin (and more often Greek) to students of high prior attainment in English and/or Modern Languages. These students were thought to be 'up to the challenge' of learning Latin and Greek. This selection by prior attainment effectively excluded the majority of learners. Research by Holmes-Henderson (2023a) into the impact of learning Latin and Greek on children's cognitive development disproved the belief that they should be the preserve of 'gifted and talented' or 'more able' students. In fact, the three groups of students whose progress increased significantly were those who speak English as an additional language, those with special education needs and disabilities and those who qualify for free school meals. The era of limiting access to the study of Classics must end. It perpetuates the elitist perception of Classics and creates a false binary.

## To teach prose composition (or not)?

Prose composition, or writing Latin and Greek sentences or passages, is an option in language assessments. It is not compulsory for students at school to take this option but some teachers (and academics) believe that it is beneficial for students to generate Latin text because it requires them to consolidate their knowledge of accidence and grammar. Some university Classics courses do not require students to do prose composition, so trainee Classics teachers can find themselves feeling daunted at the prospect of teaching a new skill. Methods and activities to teach prose composition are discussed in chapter 4.

## Relevance in the 21st-century curriculum

At a time when Science, Technology, Engineering and Mathematics (STEM) are being prioritised by government, questions continue to be asked about the relevance and value of arts and humanities subjects in young people's education. Classics, of course, suffers from allegations of being nothing but the study of 'dead languages', or indeed 'dead white men'.

Within and beyond the Classics community, there is concern about how Classics has been used as a tool for empire building, inextricably linked to colonialism. Classicists have questioned whether we should 'burn it all down' (Zuckerberg, 2019), 'cancel Classics' and allow Classical Reception Studies to rebuild a more responsible version of the subject for study in schools. For further reading on this, see (among others) Hanink (2021), Poser (2021) and Umachandran and Ward (2023). We will explore in chapter 2 what Classics teachers are doing to address some of these issues.

# What can research tell us about Classics teaching?

Classics lags behind other curriculum subjects in terms of an established research base for pedagogy, policy and practice. Classics education remains on the periphery of academic research in both Classics and education. There is one dedicated Research Centre for Classics Education in the UK (at Durham University), launched by founder director Professor Holmes-Henderson in 2024. It is hoped that more UK universities will create pathways for master's and doctoral students to study topics in Classics education to grow the evidence base and raise the profile of this emerging field. In the early stages, this will involve asking practising Classics teachers to co-supervise and/or examine students' dissertations, because there is a paucity of academic posts that have Classics education research in their remit. The authors suggest that collaboration with experienced educators will facilitate knowledge exchange and improve the quality of education for diversely positioned stakeholders across the Classics community. For Classics to catch up with disciplines such as Modern Languages, Mathematics and English, which have established chairs in subject-specific education and pedagogy, we must value teachers' expertise and experience.

We provide three examples of recent research.

## Example 1: access to Classics in schools

**Publication:** Hunt, S. and Holmes-Henderson, A. (2021) 'A level Classics poverty. Classical subjects in schools in England: Access, attainment and progression', *Council of University Classical Departments Bulletin*, 50, pp. 1–26. (https://cucd.blogs.sas.ac.uk/files/2021/02/Holmes-Henderson-and-Hunt-Classics-Poverty.docx.pdf)

In 2021, Steven Hunt and Arlene Holmes-Henderson published a landmark article titled 'A level Classics Poverty: Classical subjects in schools in England: Access, attainment and progression'. They revealed huge geographical gaps in the UK where students cannot access any classical subjects at A-level. Even in schools where the subjects are offered, they demonstrated, using Department for Education data, that classical subjects are fragile: the majority of classes consist of five or fewer students. The authors defined this lack of access to schools that offer classical subjects at A-level and earlier as 'classics poverty'. This article examines each classical subject in turn, providing student numbers, school types and school locations and uncovers grade disparities between Classics and other qualification subjects. This research informed the delivery of the Department for Education's £4m Latin Excellence Programme (where the focus is on growing Latin and Classics in schools outside London, South East and East of England).

## Example 2: Latin and literacy

**Publication (a):** Holmes-Henderson, A. and Kelly, K. (2023) 'Learn the root. Conquer the word. Investigating the efficacy of *Vocabulous* in teaching word roots', Christ Church Research Centre. (www.chch.ox.ac.uk/sites/default/files/2023-12/Vocabulous-report-Holmes-Henderson-December-2023.pdf)

**Publication (b):** Wright, P. (2023) 'Including the excluded: Teaching Latin in an area of high socio-economic disadvantage', in Holmes-Henderson, A. (ed.) *Expanding Classics: Practitioner Perspectives from Museums and Schools.* Routledge, pp. 30–41.

**Publication (c):** Holmes-Henderson, A. (2023a) 'Ancient languages for 6- to 11-year-olds: Exploring three pedagogical approaches via a longitudinal study', in Holmes-Henderson, A. (ed.) *Expanding Classics: Practitioner Perspectives from Museums and Schools.* Routledge, pp. 8–29.

These studies examine the relationship between learning Latin or Greek and English literacy.

Publication (a) focuses on learners aged 9–14 who trialled the use of an EdTech platform to deepen their knowledge of English word roots based on Latin and Greek. The outcomes demonstrated improved recognition and use of new vocabulary, as well as increased confidence in working out the meaning of unfamiliar words.

Publication (b) asked 'What impact does the teaching of Latin have on vocabulary development for Year 6 pupils in Blackpool?' The literacy attainment of 160 Year 6 students was monitored as they prepared for their SATs. Of the 160, 26% qualified for the pupil premium grant. Another local school agreed to their Year 6 cohort being used as a control group. The control-group students were not exposed to any Latin teaching during the study. The control school had a similar level of children who qualified for pupil premium, which was important when analysing the results. Finally, all children at the schools involved in the research had no prior formal Latin education. The study revealed that boys made significant progress. Overall, 73% of males involved in the project improved their understanding of the Latin words selected and the link to the English tier 2 words derived from Latin. Students were tested on their knowledge of the Latin words encountered (through matching translation tasks) but, crucially, in their ability to match definitions of the English word derived from the Latin. Overall, 64% of females saw an improvement in the accuracy of their understanding of the tier 2 English words and 56% of children who qualify as pupil premium recipients improved their scores on average by 25%. It is clear that just 45 minutes of Latin per week over 17 weeks had substantial vocabulary benefits for students. These small-scale research findings indicate that there is a positive correlation between learning Latin and student understanding of English vocabulary with Latinate roots.

Publication (c) communicates findings of a longitudinal study into the impact of learning Latin and Greek on primary school children's cognitive development. Groundbreaking in its research design, scope and scale, it presents data that disprove long-held assumptions about who benefits most from learning ancient languages in school. For decades, access to Latin in British classrooms has been restricted to those whose intellectual capacity was considered sufficient to cope with the demands of the language (Quigley, 2018, p. 62). Students who excelled in English or modern languages were 'allowed' to learn Latin as a means to stretch and deepen their literacy skills. Those who excelled at Latin were permitted to learn ancient Greek. Over five years, Holmes-Henderson gathered quantitative and qualitative data from more than 2000 students and teachers which demonstrate that Latin unlocks the most significant literacy gains for students who are performing below age-related literacy expectations. In many cases, these were young people who speak English as an additional language, have special educational needs or come from socio-economically disadvantaged backgrounds and are eligible for free school meals: the same learners who have been excluded from learning Latin and Greek in the past. Findings indicated that learning Latin had a positive impact on student outcomes in English etymology, morphology and semantics. There were improvements across reading and writing assessments for participants in the study.

### Example 3: Ancient History and social justice

**Publication:** Foster, F. and Wise, J. (2022) 'Social tensions in studying Ancient History', *The Curriculum Journal*, 33(4), pp. 536–552.

This article reports on the findings of an investigation into the tensions perceived by students aged 14–15 studying Ancient History in England, between their interest in the ancient world itself and the status of Ancient History as a curriculum subject. Foster and Wise use Young's distinction between powerful knowledge and knowledge of the powerful as a critical tool. The empirical data arise from an interview study across three different school communities in England of 14–15-year-old students studying Ancient History as a curriculum subject. Across the three schools, 32 students took part in the interview study. Students focused on the ancient world's personal relevance to their own lives. They also ascribed value not just to expertise about the ancient world but to understanding how others responded to it. However, the students all felt that studying Ancient History was a sign of an elite and privileged education, an image with which they did not feel entirely comfortable.

# CHAPTER 2
# WHAT DOES CLASSICS TEACHING LOOK LIKE?

## What is at the core and in the hinterland of Classics teaching?

The appeal of Classics for many is the breadth and range of subject disciplines, time periods, geographical locations and cultures that are embraced by the title. The focus of the canon in the GCSE and A-level classical qualifications, what we call here the core, remains the history, language and culture of Greece and Rome from the eighth century BC to the second century AD, with particular focus on Athens in the fifth century BC and Rome in the first century BC and first century AD.

There is some scope within the current specifications to go beyond this into the hinterland, but this remains limited owing to a lack of resources and the time pressure on teachers to complete the syllabus. Nevertheless, we will explore the options available and suggest how students can be introduced to the classical world beyond the Greek and Roman focus of the examination syllabuses.

### Core

#### Latin

The core authors at both GCSE and A-level from which unseens and set texts are taken do not vary greatly year on year. The set text passages in the OCR GCSE are chosen from the Oxford and Cambridge Anthologies, which include passages from Tacitus, Pliny, Suetonius, Ovid and Catullus, or they are taken directly from Virgil's *Aeneid*. The Eduqas GCSE thematic literature module offers a greater range of authors, with each topic including around eight authors, most commonly Cicero, Suetonius, Seneca, Pliny, Virgil, Ovid, Martial, Catullus and Horace. The topic choices for the culture modules at GCSE are based on core aspects of daily life in the Roman world:

| OCR | Eduqas |
|---|---|
| Romans in Britain | Roman Britain |
| Entertainment | Entertainment and leisure |
| Myths and beliefs | Roman religion |
| | Daily life in a Roman town |
| | The city of Rome |

The set text authors at A-level are predominantly Cicero, Tacitus, Livy, Virgil and Ovid, with additional options of authors such as Apuleius, Pliny, Horace and Juvenal given for the group 2 text. The prose comprehension text in the unseen language paper tends to be from an author who is less familiar to students, with recent passages taken from Quintilian, Aulus Gellius, Pliny and Velleius Paterculus.

### Greek

As with Latin, the Greek GCSE and A-level authors do not vary greatly. At GCSE, there is a limited choice of authors, with set text options taken from Herodotus, Lucian, Plato, Xenophon, Homer and Euripides. The topic choices in the culture module are 'Women in Ancient Greece', 'Athenian Society' and 'The Olympic Games'.

The main authors at A-level are Thucydides, Plato, Herodotus, Xenophon, Plutarch, Homer, Sophocles, Euripides and Aristophanes. Again, the prose comprehension texts are chosen from less familiar authors, such as Andocides, Aeschines, Hyperides, Isocrates and Lysias.

### Classical Civilisation

GCSE Classical Civilisation focuses on the core time periods of Greece and Rome: the Homeric world, Athens and Sparta in the fifth and fourth centuries BC and Rome in the first century BC and first century AD. Each module compares Greek and Roman literature and culture in five topic areas: 'Myth and Religion', 'Women in the Ancient World', 'The Homeric World', 'Roman City Life' and 'War and Warfare'.

The options open up more at A-level and there is a greater variety of modules to choose from, organised into three topic areas: 'The World of the Hero', 'Culture and the Arts' and 'Beliefs and Ideas'. The majority of modules continue to focus on the same core periods of Greek and Roman history and literature as studied at GCSE. However, there is more scope to go beyond this, as two modules include topics that fall outside the chronology and geography of the core. The module 'Invention of the Barbarian' covers the Persians, the Amazons and Medea, allowing the study of historical and mythological non-Greek people. Furthermore, the poetry of Sappho, a female poet from late seventh-century Lesbos, is studied in the 'Love and Relationships' module.

### Ancient History

Both the GCSE and A-level Ancient History courses have wider core content in terms of the geographical locations and time periods studied. At GCSE the compulsory modules are on the Persian Empire and the foundations of Rome up to 440BC. The Greek side of the course has optional modules on sixth- and fifth-century BC Athenian history and on Alexander the Great. The optional Roman modules look at Hannibal and the Second Punic War, Cleopatra and Roman Britain.

The A-level course is focused on the same core period as the Classical Civilisation course. The compulsory modules cover Greece in the fifth century BC and Rome in the late first century BC and first century AD. The optional Greek modules again focus on Athens and Sparta in the fifth century BC, with an option to study the rise of Macedon in the fourth century BC. The Roman side of the course gives the option to study the breakdown of the late Republic, the Flavians or Roman Britain.

## Hinterland

As we have seen, the GCSE and A-level specifications are focused predominantly on the history and culture of fifth-century BC Greece and first-century BC and first-century AD Rome, and on the male authors who wrote the majority of our extant sources. However, there is rich material to be studied beyond this, either as stand-alone topics in their own right or in extension to the main syllabus.

The Persian Empire is perhaps most widely taught as an extension of the Greco-Roman world, especially as it can be studied as part of the Ancient History GCSE and Classical Civilisation/Ancient History A-level. A number of schools also include it in their KS3 Classics or History curriculum, as a way to introduce students to a more varied antiquity and prepare them for the GCSE and A-level courses (McOmish, 2023). A number of useful resources are available for those who want to introduce Persia to their curriculum. The British Museum produced educational resources for their exhibition *Luxury and Power: Persia to Greece*, which can be adapted for lessons. Other easily available resources on Persia include the textbook and online teachers' handbook published by Hands Up Education.

Other areas that could be studied include the ancient Near East or Egypt. However, as it is harder to find resources for these subject areas that are appropriate for secondary students, lesson preparation becomes more onerous, further exacerbated by the fact that these subject areas may be less familiar to teachers. A bank of resources on the ancient Near East has been collated by Dr Tiffany Earley-Spadoni at the University of Central Florida. The British Museum also has a series of resources for ancient Egypt which are aimed at KS2 students but could be adapted for use at secondary level.

However, the hinterland for Classics extends beyond the geographical. The study of women's lives and the treatment of enslaved people offers an opportunity to extend students' knowledge of the ancient world beyond the largely male elite view of the prescribed sources. The publication of the *Suburani* textbook and the updated fifth edition of the *Cambridge Latin Course* have sought to address some of the gender and status imbalances in how Roman lives were portrayed in earlier Latin textbooks. Several modules in the current specifications at GCSE and A-level, for example 'Greek Theatre' and 'The World of the Hero' in A-level Classical Civilisation, include the representation of women and enslaved people as subtopics but these are relatively minor areas of study within the whole course. To go beyond this, students could be introduced to female writers such as Sappho, Praxilla, Erinna and Sulpicia. A list of female authors has been compiled by Sententiae Antiquae, a Classicist active on social media, for International Women's Day.

**Links:** Hands Up Education (https://hands-up-education.org)

*Investigating Civilisations: Persia – Teachers' handbook* (www.the-persians.co.uk/persiaTG/index.htm)

*Luxury and Power: Persia to Greece* (https://britishmuseum.org/exhibitions/luxury-and-power-persia-greece)

Open Educational Resources for the Ancient Near East, University of Central Florida (https://stars.library.ucf.edu/ancientneareast/)

Ancient Egypt, British Museum (www.britishmuseum.org/learn/schools/ages-7-11/ancient-egypt#student-resources)

List of women authors from ancient Greece and Rome for International Women's Day, Sententiae Antiquae (https://sententiaeantiquae.com/2021/03/08/a-list-of-women-authors-from-ancient-greece-and-rome-for-internationalwomensday/)

### TED-Ed

TED-Ed videos are an easy way to integrate the hinterland into the curriculum. There is a vast range of cartoons and videos on subjects on the periphery of the classical world that can be used to compare and contrast the traditional Classics curriculum. A suggested list can be accessed through the QR code.

### Training for teachers

There are several courses for teachers who want to widen their subject knowledge beyond the core discipline and, in turn, expand the study of Classics in their schools. For example, summer schools on ancient philosophy and ancient languages are held annually at universities in London and Oxford:

- Hittite, Sumerian, Sanskrit, Biblical Hebrew and Byzantine Greek (www.ucl.ac.uk/classics/open-days-outreach/summer-schools/london-summer-school-classics-2024)
- Ancient Philosophy (www.ucl.ac.uk/classics/open-days-outreach/summer-schools/ucl-summer-school-ancient-philosophy-2024)
- Anatolian languages and linguistics (www.torch.ox.ac.uk/event/anatolian-languages-and-linguistics-summer-school)

## Inclusive Classics

As discussed in chapter 1, in relation to debates within the Classics community, many teachers and academics have been striving to make the ancient world more critical and representative. Here we give several examples of the great work being done to make Classics a more inclusive discipline.

# Case study of trauma-informed teaching of Latin stories

## Peter Swallow, Durham University

Although I am now an academic, I was formerly a high-school teacher of Classics, and Head of Department. Teaching KS3 Latin with *de Romanis 1* and *2*, my department and I were faced with two particularly challenging stories: in *de Romanis 1*, the 'Theft of the Sabine Women' (as it is euphemistically called) and in *de Romanis 2*, the 'Rape of Lucretia'. Teaching these stories to Years 8 and 9, respectively, at an all-girls independent school, we were faced with three options:

1 Decide they are too difficult and skip them.

2 Teach them as presented in the book, with no modifications made to our teaching practice.

3 Adapt our teaching practice to ensure we are teaching these stories in a trauma-informed way.

Given the nature of these stories and the context in which they were to be delivered, we decided on the third approach.

The decision to skip these stories altogether seemed to us a form of sanitisation of the ancient world, which, for all its virtues, was a brutal period of history, particularly for women. It did not seem right to ignore or erase the fact that sexual violence plays such a major part in ancient myth. Perhaps we would not have included these stories in the textbook if we had been writing it, but the fact was that these stories *were* in the book and skipping over them would be noticed by the students – and it would be as if we were skipping over the existence of sexual violence. These lessons were delivered shortly after the tragic events surrounding the abduction and murder of Sarah Everard by police office Wayne Couzens, a news story widely known by our students, so we were particularly eager not to be seen to be covering up the lived reality of women.

With that in mind we were keen to adopt best practice to ensure we were teaching these challenging texts in as safe an environment as possible. Our practice here was heavily influenced by the work of Caroline Bristow, who has spoken extensively about her own experience with trauma-informed practice.

Our approach was as follows:

- We provided content warnings and made it clear that any students who found the content difficult could step out of the lesson if they needed to.
- We taught the stories in English first, so that there would be no surprises for the students.
- We made it clear that we were talking about sexual assault – not 'theft' – and discussed with students the power structures underpinning the stories and the emotional responses of the women in the stories to their trauma. It was important that our students could develop empathy for the victims' responses without shaming them for the ways in which they acted.
- We finally looked at the Latin text and worked on it as a class. I am usually a strong proponent of call-upon questioning in my lessons, but for these classes I avoided it and let students actively offer to contribute. I only wanted students to engage with the texts to the level that they felt emotionally able.
- We decided against follow-up work on these stories – we wanted the sessions spent on these texts to have a sense of closure and did not want to risk drawing out the engagement with such challenging material.

I cannot say for certain the effect that addressing these texts in this way had on my students. What I can say is that I was very impressed with the mature way in which they engaged in the lesson. While a class of Year 8 or Year 9 Latinists can usually be expected to be quite chatty, for these classes, there was a much more subdued atmosphere as they worked through the Latin. But they quickly returned to their usual boisterous selves as the lessons moved on and we left these challenging – but, I think, worthwhile – stories behind.

## Further resources

Caroline Bristow talking about trauma-informed practice: www.cambridge.org/ki/education/blog/2020/12/07/breaking-silence-confronting-sexual-violence-in-classical-myths-and-stories/

Swallow, P. (2023) 'Teaching difficult stories. Trauma-informed teaching in the Classics classroom', *Journal of Classics Teaching*, 24(48), pp. 162–164.

## Case study of the Inclusive Classics Unseens Project

Gráinne Cassidy, education coordinator for the Classical Association

This project was inspired by the Inclusive Classics conference in July 2020 and Dr Amy Coker's own frustrations with the limitations of off-the-shelf teaching materials for GCSE Latin, which have an overwhelming focus on political and military themes or are adaptations of myths – meaning women and girls rarely have their own autonomous voices. Amy, along with 20 volunteer teachers, began developing a suite of teaching materials for GCSE Latin that would broaden the horizons of students to the greater social, geographical and cultural variety of the ancient world beyond the usual canon and topics towards which the GCSE (and A-level) qualifications in Latin are geared, including marginalised groups.

These passages are either Latin texts reworked for GCSE level or creative pieces inspired by ancient texts and artefacts. However, the limited vocabulary on the Defined Vocabulary List at GCSE and its focus on military and political vocabulary has proved an interesting challenge to overcome. Each passage is intended to spark classroom conversation at the same time as students are practising language work: most teachers have little or no time to spend on activities not directly related to the GCSE qualification, and unseen practice seemed to be a good way of integrating additional material.

Alongside these stories, this suite of resources will also include discussion questions and freely available supplementary reading material that will enable both teachers and students to explore the topics and themes covered in the passages. These passages are designed to be useful to both the OCR and Eduqas specifications and are formatted according to guidance from Asterion (see p. 31) to ensure that they is as accessible as possible to a wide range of learners. While there are a plethora of different themes, texts and artefacts that could be included in this project, we hope that this initial suite of resources will provide new opportunities for contemporary conversations in the Latin classroom. This project is now under the aegis of the Classical Association, which will further develop, host and promote these freely accessible resources. Sign up to the Classical Association Education Bulletin to find out more (see 'Organisations' on p. 120).

### Queering the Past(s)

Queering the Past(s) is an interactive online resource that has been developed by a team of teachers and scholars to address an important gap in school education on LGBTQ+ subjects. It uses information from antiquity to help students gain confidence in addressing modern critical (and contentious) issues. Digital e-books, lessons and activities on Sappho, Elagabalus and the Amazons are free-to-download resources on the website. Teachers and students can use these to explore LGBTQ+ identities and issues in a range of subject lessons such as English, History and Classics as well as Relationships and Sex Education (RSE). Equally, they could be used by LGBTQ+ student groups and as part of a school-wide celebration of LGBT History month (February) or Pride month (June).

**Link:** https://classicalassociation.org/queering-the-past/

### Asterion

Asterion is an organisation run by neurodivergent people in Classics. Their goals are to raise the profile of neurodiversity, celebrate the achievements of neurodivergent classicists and tackle barriers to inclusion. To do so, their website hosts resources and a blog to provide support and training.

**Link:** https://asterion.uk/

## What different forms can KS3 Classics curricula take?

The teaching of GCSE and A-level classical subjects is prescribed by the exam board specifications, leaving little opportunity for originality and creativity in developing the subject content of curricula at this level. However, as Classics is not included in the national curriculum, there are no such restrictions at KS3. The main requirement at these levels is to sufficiently prepare students so they can start the GCSE course(s) offered. For schools that teach Latin in KS3 in preparation for GCSE, their curriculum plan will most likely be tied to the order in which the textbook they use introduces grammar and para-linguistic material. Schools that focus on Classics at KS3 have more freedom to choose which topics and subject content they teach, as there is no required prior knowledge to start GCSE Ancient History and Classical Civilisation. However, most schools that teach KS3 Classics introduce their students to the core of Greek and Roman history and culture to provide a grounding for the GCSE syllabuses.

The three most common models for teaching classical subjects at GCSE are explored below, with suggestions given for subject content and resources that might be used. However, there is not one definitive or optimal curriculum model and schools might utilise elements of all three. Teachers must choose the format that works best for students and their school contexts.

## School One – Classics club at lunchtime

In many schools where classical subjects are not on the curriculum, non-specialist teachers with a passion for the subject run Classics clubs at lunchtime. Predominantly aimed at KS3 students, these clubs are an opportunity to engage students who would otherwise not receive any formal tuition in the culture, language and literature of the ancient world. A Classics club not only enriches the students' knowledge and understanding of Classics but can also develop their skills of enquiry, creativity and critical thinking. For this reason, many schools that do have Classics on the curriculum may also run Classics clubs, as they are a great way to develop students' interest in the ancient world.

The choice of topics and type of materials used depends on the experience and confidence of the teacher running the club. An example structure that includes a mix of history and literature might be as follows:

**Year 1:**

Term one – Ancient Greece

Term two – Ovid's *Metamorphoses*

Term three – creative response project to either topic

**Year 2:**

Term one – Amarantus Project (daily life in Pompeii)

Term two – Homer's *Iliad*

Term three – creative response project to either topic

**Year 3:**

Term one – The Persians

Term two – Homer's *Odyssey*

Term three – creative response project to either topic

A more detailed outline and suggested resources can be accessed through the QR code.

The Olympus Challenge run by Classics for All is one way to recognise the work completed by students and give structure and aim to a Classics club. The challenge is open to all students and those who complete the required components are awarded a certificate from Classics for All. Students have to complete at least three components, which include studying a cultural or historical topic, classical literature or Latin or Greek. Other options include producing a creative response to a classical topic or a presentation following a visit to a museum or classical site. The challenge can be completed within one year or over a number of years.

**Link:** Olympus Challenge poster, Classics for All (https://classicsforall.org.uk/sites/default/files/uploads/Olympus%20Challenge%20poster.pdf)

## School Two – Classics embedded in other subjects

Another option for schools that are not able to timetable classical subjects into their KS3 curriculum is to include Classics in other subject areas. This relies on good relationships between departments and non-specialist teachers who are willing to teach outside their subject area. Classics for All and other organisations provide CPD for non-specialist teachers to teach classical subjects. Even in schools that do have Classics on the curriculum, there is great value in developing inter-department links to show students that Classics has relevance for many different areas of education and to the wider world.

English and History are the subjects into which Classics is most often integrated. Selections of classical texts, such as the *Odyssey* or Ovid's *Metamorphoses*, could be studied in English. Modules of Ancient History could be included in the History curriculum – for example, the Persians or Romans could be studied to explore an example of empire, or the Roman conquest could be used to investigate the political, military and social history of ancient Britain. Alongside English and History, other subject areas into which Classics could be integrated are:

- Art – representations of mythology, vases, orders of architecture

- Biology – etymology to enrich student understanding of key vocabulary, plants
- Chemistry – names of elements that derive from Latin
- Citizenship – democracy, rights and responsibilities, rhetoric
- Design and technology – Roman weapons, heating
- Maths – Roman numerals
- Drama – Aristotle's theory of drama, Greek (and Roman) comedies and tragedies
- Modern Languages – Romance language cognates
- Music – *Dido and Aeneas*, other Classics-inspired music
- PE – the Olympic Games
- Philosophy – Plato, Aristotle, pre-Socratics
- Physics – constellations
- Religious Studies – pantheistic religions.

Resources that may be of interest include:

- Citizenship/English – *Approaches to Rhetoric* (https://englishandmedia.co.uk/publications-magazines/20711/emc-approaches-to-rhetoric-a-practical-introduction-for-11-14-emc-free-download/)
- History – *Amarantus Project* (https://cambridgeamarantus.com/home)
- Maths – Roman numerals (https://segedunumromanfort.org.uk/know-your-numbers-roman-numerals)
- Philosophy – *Delphi the Philosopher* (www.delphi-philosophy.com/1-the-trial-of-socrates)
- Physics – *The Science of Stories* (www.bristol.ac.uk/classics/hub/for-schools/the-science-of-stories/)

The following case studies demonstrate how Classics can be integrated into KS3 English and History curricula. Mariyam Batka suggests the many benefits that teaching classical texts, such as Homer's *Odyssey*, can bring to English lessons and Anna McOmish explains how she included Ancient History in the History curriculum.

# Case study of teaching Classics in KS3 English
Mariyam Batka, Woldingham School

The proposal to teach classical texts as part of the English curriculum can evoke a mixed response from English teachers. Sceptics raise valid concerns, including worries about the lack of diversity within these texts and the portrayal of women in many of the stories. They also point out potential challenges, such as the added cognitive load arising from the unique contextual and historical details of each text, confusion regarding which version or translation to use, and arguments about other texts having higher priority in terms of links to later learning.

While I do not claim to have all the answers to the aforementioned issues, I strongly believe that classical texts have a place within the English curriculum. They can be used to teach students about diversity, equip them with the tools needed to analyse texts they will encounter at GCSE, A-level and beyond in a more meaningful way, and provide them with a solid understanding of the significant ideas and themes present in various forms of literature. For me, the decision to include classical texts in the English curriculum must be carefully planned and rooted in a desire to create a knowledge-rich curriculum.

Although the English curriculum at GCSE is largely determined by the exam board selected, I believe that introducing Homer's *Odyssey* at KS3, particularly in Year 7, can be beneficial. Students in Year 7 may already have some familiarity with Greek mythology from primary school or through their own independent reading, but even those who have not encountered any Greek myths can engage with the almost short-story format of Odysseus' encounters and adventures with various human and mythical characters. The *Odyssey* lends itself well to both English literature and English language focuses, making it ideal for Year 7, when teachers are assessing the overall reading and writing abilities of their students.

In terms of practical teaching ideas, I have found the following to have worked well:

- Discussions and the reading of non-fiction articles about the treatment of refugees can be sparked by Odysseus' plight when he finds himself washed up on the island of the Phaeacians.

- The Greek concept of *xenia* (hospitality towards foreigners) explored within the text lends itself to creative-writing pieces centred around the theme of hospitality and entertaining an unknown stranger.

- Odysseus' encounter with Circe provides an opportunity to explore the portrayal of women in literature and I have used it to create a courtroom-like debate, with one side defending her actions and the other prosecuting her.
- At the end of the unit, students can be given the task to create an *Odyssey* board game. In the past, classes have produced some brilliant work in response to this and it enables them to consolidate their understanding of the key events in the storyline.

Teaching the *Odyssey* at KS3 can lay the groundwork required for analysing *Macbeth* as a GCSE text, with ample opportunities for students to recall and build upon the knowledge and big ideas gained at KS3, including the impact of supernatural forces on the storyline, the weird sisters and portrayal of Lady Macbeth relating to the presentation of women in the *Odyssey*, revisiting the concept of *xenia* to understand interactions between characters, and to fully grasp Macbeth's internal conflict in Act 1, Scene 7.

Other ideas with a Classics origin that can be included in the English curriculum are teaching Aristotle's rhetoric at KS3, which helps students to understand speeches and propaganda and aids them in developing their own persuasive writing. Additionally, looking at words with a Latin origin as part of a unit on introduction to language at KS3 can help students decode the meaning of unfamiliar vocabulary, making them more confident and independent readers.

### Further resources

Bloor, A., McCabe, M. and Holmes-Henderson, A. (2023) 'Using classical mythology to teach English as an Additional Language', in Holmes-Henderson, A. (ed.) *Expanding Classics*, Routledge.

Stealth Classics video from the Classical Association (https://vimeo.com/653622576)

# Case study of including Ancient History in the KS3 curriculum

## Anna McOmish, Haybridge High School, formerly Aldridge School

Aldridge School educates approximately 1600 students, aged 11–18 in Walsall, West Midlands, of whom 34% have been eligible for free school meals in the last six years, which is significantly above the national average. GCSE Ancient History was introduced in 2017 and the KS3 curriculum was adapted in the summer term of 2019 to include an Ancient History topic in each KS3 year group, lasting half a term each (approximately six to eight weeks). Below is the KS3 History curriculum at Aldridge School with changes from summer 2019 highlighted in bold.

| Year Seven | Year Eight | Year Nine |
|---|---|---|
| Norman Conquest | English Civil War | **Ancient Middle East** |
| Medieval Kings | Industrial Revolution | Origins of First World War |
| Medieval Life | Atlantic Slave Trade | First World War/Interwar years |
| Wars of the Roses | British Empire | Second World War |
| Tudor Life | Civil Rights Movement | Nazi Germany |
| **Ancient Greece** | **Ancient Rome** | The Cold War |

Including Ancient History relating to fifth-century BC Greece, Rome 753BC–AD476 and the ancient Middle East 3000BC–479BC in our KS3 curriculum ensured that the content students needed to know for Ancient History GCSE (and A-level) was being introduced in simple forms from which students could generalise the information for reuse later in their studies (Bruner, 1960).

### The ancient Middle East 3000BC–479BC

The chronological range for this Year 9 unit was large, as our aim was for students to develop a clear understanding of the geography of the area and the timeline of events that led up to and included the Persian Empire depth study in the Ancient History GCSE.

The topic included 12 lessons under two enquiry questions (EQ) in the following order.

| The ancient Middle East 3000BC–479BC | EQ | Lesson title |
|---|---|---|
| | Lessons 1–4: How far was this the 'cradle of civilisation'? | The city of Ur |
| | | The new Hittite Kingdom |
| | | The Battle of Qadesh |
| | | The Sea People (Bronze Age Collapse) |
| | CHANGE OF EQ | |
| | Lessons 5–12: Which was the most successful dynasty of the ancient Middle East? | Assyria: Ashurnasirpal II |
| | | Assyria: Tiglath-Pileser II |
| | | Assyria: Ashurbanipal |
| | | Assyria to Babylon |
| | | Babylon: Nebuchadnezzar |
| | | Persia: Cyrus the Great |
| | | Persia: Cambyses II |
| | | Persia: Darius I |

*EQ1 – How far was this the 'cradle of civilisation'?*
Taking inspiration from Stephen Bourke's *The Middle East: The Cradle of Civilization Revealed* (2008), this EQ introduced students to evidence that has helped create the idea of the area being the 'cradle of civilisation'. The EQ surveyed major events up until the Bronze Age collapse around 1200BC, which allowed students to assess the validity of this idea.

Subsequent lessons gave an overview of the kings of the new Hittite dynasty, focusing on the accession and achievements of each king. Students concentrated on comparative work between the kings and built upon the idea that the area created strongly led and 'civilised' kingdoms. The final lessons within the EQ investigated the Bronze Age collapse of 1200BC. Initially focusing on the Sea Peoples, the first lesson studied the origins and consequences of the Bronze Age collapse, analysing ancient sources such as the letter from Ugarit and the Egyptian relief of the Battle of the Delta to understand contemporary ideas about the causes of the collapse. The second lesson used modern interpretations to understand recent hypotheses behind the collapse, leading students to assess how far the area was 'the cradle of civilisation' if this event could have such devastating consequences.

*EQ2 – Which was the most successful dynasty of the ancient Middle East?*
The second EQ analysed the characteristics and achievements of the most significant dynasties of the ancient Middle East, ending with a study of the first three Achaemenid kings, which is compulsory in the Ancient History GCSE. Considering the Neo-Assyrians, the Babylonians and the Achaemenids, this EQ enabled students to develop skills of analysis and evaluation by comparing dynasties under their own definition of 'success' and to draw thematic comparisons with other areas of the KS3 curriculum. Themes such as nation-building, empire, kingship and warfare were present in the unit and had also been discussed at various points throughout Year 7 and Year 8.

The first lessons covered the Neo-Assyrian kings and were popular with students. These lessons assessed the origins of the Assyrians, how far Ashurnasirpal II was a pragmatist or a megalomaniac, the expansion under Tiglath-Pileser II, the importance of his wife, Queen Yaba. The lessons ended with studying Ashurbanipal and his approach to education and state-building. These lessons were rich in material culture and evaluated the successes of the Assyrians as well as various factors that led to the fall of Assyria and the rise of Babylon/King Nabopolassar. The final lessons of the unit looked at Cyrus the Great, Cambyses II and Darius I. In these lessons, students consistently used ancient sources, such as Herodotus, the Cyrus Cylinder and the Bisitun Inscription.

## Assessment

This unit's assessment centred on an essay-style question that asked students to use their own knowledge and ancient sources to respond to the question: '"Ashurnasirpal was the most successful of the ancient Middle Eastern kings". How far do you agree with this statement?' It was a response to this assessment question that sparked my interest in researching student perceptions of this unit and particularly the responses of Muslim students. An Asian male Muslim student in my class, whom I had taught since Year 8 and who had shown average engagement until Year 9, completed this assessment and handed to me a four-page, informed and compellingly argued response as to why Ashurbanipal was the most successful of the ancient Middle Eastern kings. It remains to this day one of the most enjoyable assessments I have ever read.

> **Impacts**
> 1 Muslim students reported that they felt more 'successful' in Ancient History lessons than in other history topics. The majority of students also rated their 'success' highly.
> 2 Muslim students felt a greater sense of connection and belonging in lessons, when learning about the ancient Middle East.
> 3 Black students were highly positive about, and engaged by, the topic.
> 4 Ancient history holds particular value among students because it helps them to understand causation and consequence in human history.

To learn more about Anna's introduction of Ancient History at KS3, read her chapter 'Promoting inclusivity through teaching Ancient History' (2023) in *Expanding Classics* (Holmes-Henderson, 2023b).

## School Three – Latin or Classics on the curriculum

The provision in schools that do have Latin or Classics on the curriculum in KS3 can vary greatly in terms of which year groups the subjects are available to (or compulsory for), how many periods a week they are taught, and whether all students get to study both Latin and Classics or just one of them. Moreover, in some schools only part of the cohort are invited to learn Latin, either based on prior attainment in English or modern languages (setting) or as a result of timetabling restrictions between classes.

### Latin

The curriculum often depends on the textbook used and how it introduces grammar and cultural material. Two popular textbooks are the *Cambridge Latin Course* and *Suburani*, both based on the reading method. Others used in schools that prefer the grammar–translation method are *de Romanis*, Taylor's *Latin to GCSE* and the out-of-print Oxford Latin Course.

Depending on their timetable allocation and nature of their cohorts, schools typically attempt to teach five or six chapters per year in KS3. Schemes of work usually focus on the teaching of Latin language to develop competence and fluency in reading comprehension and translation. However, the cultural background material remains an important part of developing students' interest in, and understanding of, life in ancient Rome or Pompeii. This aids their comprehension of Latin stories and provides an excellent foundational knowledge for the study of Classical Civilisation and Ancient History, so it should not be ignored.

## Classics

Classics is not included in the KS3 national curriculum in England. As already discussed in chapter 1, this absence of classical subjects from the statutory requirements for the KS3 curriculum has led to 'Classics poverty' in many schools and areas of the country (Hunt and Holmes-Henderson, 2021). Nevertheless, it leaves schools that do include Classics in their curricula with the freedom to develop bespoke courses to suit their students. In the following case study, Gem Adams explains how her department approached the task of developing an engaging curriculum that both introduced students to the core traditions of the discipline and also provided scope for wider debate.

## Case study of KS3 Classical Civilisation curriculum
### Gem Adams, Allerton Grange School

In 2020, Allerton Grange School introduced Classical Civilisation to the curriculum at KS3. With no tradition of teaching Classics at KS3, we had *carte blanche* to design a curriculum from scratch.

The first step in designing our Classics curriculum was deciding what the powerful core knowledge is within our subject discipline. This is the knowledge that we want students to retain in their long-term memory and will provide the building blocks for all future learning and new information. Deciding on the core knowledge that would underpin our curriculum took a lot of lengthy conversations and debates in departmental meetings. There are some traditions of the discipline that we could not compromise on. For example, we do not want students to leave KS3 not knowing who Homer was and being able to name the epics he (probably) composed. Other traditions caused a lot more debate, did we consider the Labours of Heracles to be core knowledge? After much careful consideration we settled on the following.

### Core knowledge

1 The Greek and Roman pantheon

2 The make-up of the ancient world (geography and chronology)

3 The reciprocal relationship between gods and mortals

4 The myth of the Judgement of Paris

5 The Trojan War

6 Homer's *Iliad* and *Odyssey*

7 The concept of a hero

8 The foundation of Rome

9 Roman governance (monarchy, republic, empire)

10 Types of evidence and their issues

Once we had agreed on this core knowledge, we had to decide how we would map it, how knowledge would be sequenced to enable students to access new knowledge, and where this knowledge would be revisited as part of the Progression Model, which can be accessed through the QR code below.

The curriculum journey at KS3 (as well as KS4 and KS5) is layered to give students the opportunities to revisit knowledge and concepts across units. The schema that students master becomes broader and more complex each year. For example, in Year 7, students are identifying who the deities in the pantheon are and their responsibilities. In Year 8, students examine how the divine figures are represented in sculpture and their role in mythology. By Year 9, students are exploring how the deities in the pantheon are depicted in Homer and analysing anthropomorphism.

## EQs in the KS3 Curriculum

*Year 7*
How do we study the ancient world?

Why was '*rex*' such a dirty word in ancient Rome?*

*Year 8*
What was the significance of the Athenian acropolis?

How can mythology develop our understanding of Greek beliefs and society?

*Year 9*
How did an apple cause the Trojan War?

What did it mean to be a Homeric hero?

To what extent are the Romans Italian?

Before planning these EQs, we decided on the substantive knowledge, hinterland knowledge, disciplinary knowledge and the subject-specific vocabulary that we wanted students to encounter and learn within the unit. We also considered which scholarly debates exist within academia that could be incorporated into, and used to shape, these enquiries. For example, the EQ 'Why was "*rex*" such a dirty word in ancient Rome?' is based on the scholarship of Mary Beard in *SPQR* (2016). Scholarship on Virgil's *Aeneid* by R. Deryck Williams (2009) is the basis for the Year 9 enquiry, 'To what extent are the Romans Italian?'

The work of the curriculum is never done and as subject experts we will continue to carefully consider and develop our KS3 curriculum.

*The scheme of learning and resources for 'Why was "rex" such a dirty word in ancient Rome?' are available in full on the Classics for All Resources Hub* (https://resources.classicsforall.org.uk/key-stage-3/why-was-rex-such-dirty-word-ancient-rome)

# CHAPTER 3
# HOW CAN INSTRUCTIONAL TEACHING BE USED IN CLASSICS?

## What is Mode A and Mode B teaching?

Mode A and Mode B teaching are terms first used by Tom Sherrington in *The Learning Rainforest* (2017) to distinguish between instructional teaching and more creative and independent classroom activities. The majority of lesson time is likely to be spent on Mode A, particularly when students are new to a subject or topic, as it is vital for building schemata and developing fluency. Nevertheless, Mode B is an important part of motivating and engaging students and of developing a wider set of skills.

| Mode A | Mode B |
|---|---|
| Explain | Exploration |
| Model | Discovery |
| Practice | Going off-piste |
| Feedback | Creative and open-ended tasks |
| Testing | Projects |
| Review | Giving choice |

In this chapter, we will give examples of techniques and activities that can be used in the Classics classroom and show where they are supported by cognitive science and pedagogical research. It is not in the scope of this book to go into the detail of these theories, as they are expertly covered by the first *In Action* series and elsewhere. Please use the QR links and references for suggested further reading.

## What does Mode A look like in Classics teaching?

Mode A is the day-to-day teaching tasks of instruction, modelling and practice. It requires responsive teaching where the teacher engages with their class by regularly checking for understanding and adapting their approach as necessary. The teacher must therefore take a leading role in these activities. Indeed, teacher-led instruction has been shown to be more effective than minimal instruction (Kirschner et al., 2006), and student-centred instruction may even have a negative effect on academic achievement and increase educational inequality for disadvantaged students (Andersen and Andersen, 2017).

Good instruction is so vital for learning, as the constraints of working memory mean that young adults are limited to storing only three to five meaningful items at one time (Cowan, 2010). Cognitive Load Theory proposes that we can work around this limitation by optimising the intrinsic and germane load and reducing the extraneous (Lovell, 2020). In other words, we should design our curriculum and methods of instruction so that students are not distracted by irrelevant details. Teachers should ensure that tasks are appropriate for students' level of working memory. This means:

- pre-teaching material and linking it to prior knowledge
- introducing concepts in steps
- considering the sequence of instruction
- providing worked examples and model answers
- scaffolding tasks
- removing redundant information (for example, keeping vocabulary simple when the focus is on a new grammar point)
- reducing split attention (for example putting grammar tables on the same slide or page as the questions, so attention does not need to flick between different items)
- giving simplified definitions
- using dual coding.

This does not mean making instruction too easy for students, but balancing the level of information provided at a time so they can work through it successfully and build their skills, long-term memory and confidence. Then as students become more proficient and develop automation, these scaffolds and supports can be removed.

For further information about the role of working memory in language teaching, see:

Chartered College, 'Cognitive Load Theory and its application in the classroom' (https://my.chartered.college/impact_article/cognitive-load-theory-and-its-application-in-the-classroom/)

The Language Gym, 'Eight important facts about working memory and their implications for foreign-language teaching and learning' (https://gianfrancoconti.com/2015/07/05/eight-important-facts-about-working-memory-and-their-implication-of-mfl-teaching-and-learning/)

Moreover, the expertise reversal effect suggests that instruction that works for less-experienced learners can have a negative impact on those learners with more experience (Kalyuga et al., 2003). Providing more individualised instruction or opportunities for students to select their own tasks may reverse this (Kalyuga, 2007), however, individualised instruction is not possible or practical for most teachers. Teachers must therefore know their classes well and use the appropriate level of instruction based on their assessment of students' levels of competence and confidence, moving to more independent practice as students' knowledge and skill levels progress.

## Pre-teaching

Knowledge is more easily organised and integrated into long-term memory when a learner has developed schemata, a cognitive process through which they connect new information to things that they already know. Novices who do not have sufficient prior knowledge on a particular topic find learning and problem solving much more difficult than experts who have already built these connections (Chi et al., 1981). Breaking content down into small steps and pre-teaching key information allows students to develop their schemata more effectively and efficiently. Pre-teaching also allows teachers to assess what students already know and amend their teaching accordingly.

**Link:** 'A complete guide to schema theory and its role in education' (www.educationcorner.com/schema-theory/)

### Vocabulary

New vocabulary can produce a high cognitive load and make comprehension of a text more difficult. We need to know around 95% of the vocabulary of a text to understand its content (Quigley, 2018). Using the dictionary and guessing meaning from context are valuable skills for students to learn when faced with unknown words. However, they can prove to be unhelpful if they are time consuming or lead to misunderstandings (Beck et al., 2013; Scott and Nagy, 1997). Pre-teaching vocabulary can therefore make this process smoother.

For languages, vocabulary that will be encountered in a story can be introduced or reviewed first before it is read by the class. This could be done by reading through the glossed vocabulary list given alongside the text to discuss what the story might be about or by asking students to pick words out from the story that they are unfamiliar with, in order to define the meanings before starting. A vocabulary list of new or difficult words from the story could be displayed on the board and the class could discuss the meanings and possible derivatives of these words. Other vocabulary revision tasks that will be discussed later in this chapter could also be used here.

For Classical Civilisation and Ancient History, pre-teaching difficult or unfamiliar English vocabulary and technical terminology is beneficial for all students, but particularly for SEND and EAL students (Whittaker and Hayes, 2018). Alex Quigley in *Closing the Vocabulary Gap* (2018) proposes the SEEC model for explicit vocabulary teaching:

- *Select* the words to pre-teach.
- *Explain* the meaning of the words, giving a friendly definition and examples.
- *Explore* the word further, for example, its etymology, common word families or different uses in different disciplines (this stage is not always necessary or practical).
- *Consolidate* understanding through repeated exposure, using the word in different contexts, testing, further research or noting the words in a record of key vocabulary or terminology.

Regular testing of the meaning and spelling of this terminology will also be needed, so students are confident with the form and meaning of words and can use them accurately in exams. Online resources for pronunciation, such as Emily Wilson's guide to pronouncing names in the *Iliad* and *Odyssey* and the ARLT recordings of Greek and Latin literature, can be used to develop familiarity with the sounds of words and in turn their spellings and meanings.

**Links:** Pronunciation guide for the *Iliad* and *Odyssey* (www.emilyrcwilson.com/pronunciation-guide)

Recordings of Latin and Greek literature by ARLT members (www.arlt.co.uk/resources/audio-readings/)

## Cultural and historical context

The richness of the cultural and historical contexts of our subjects is a great advantage and draw for both studying and teaching Classics. Nevertheless, for students who have little prior knowledge of the ancient world, this richness adds to their cognitive load and can lead to confusion and frustration at the additional work needed to understand the content. The importance of pre-teaching and providing a level starting point for the whole class was shown by Nuthall's seminal research *The Hidden Lives of Learners* (2007). A student has to make sense of new information based on existing knowledge before they can store it in long-term memory, so their level of prior understanding can either help this process or create misconceptions.

The teacher's task is therefore to choose the quantity and depth of information they must pre-teach to their students so they can understand new material. For example, to be able to understand a story set in the Roman baths, how much do they need to understand about Roman bathing and social customs? To be able to translate and understand Cicero's *Pro Caelio*, how much do they need to know about Roman law courts and the biographies of those involved? To be able to work on the Julio-Claudian period study in A-level Ancient History, how much do they need to know about the breakdown of the Republic and the civil wars that led to Augustus' formation of the principate? The answer to each will of course depend on the class and teaching context and will change between individual cohorts, so this will need to be carefully considered by the teacher and prepared in advance.

To assess students' prior knowledge before teaching a topic, you might first start with a quiz on the the key knowledge and ideas involved in it, especially if it relates to something that students have studied before. Graphic organisers could also be used to set out key background knowledge and provide students with a frame to which they can connect new information that acts as a model for the development of their own schemata. Examples of graphic organisers are discussed later in this chapter.

## Characters

It is often difficult to keep in mind who is who in a story or text and how they are related, particularly as Greek and Roman names are unfamiliar. The characters that students meet could be historical figures or fictional characters in language textbooks and literature. Pre-teaching and reminders of who characters are can improve students' understanding and make it easier for them to encounter new information. Oliver Lovell suggests that one of the best ways is through a character map (2020). It is standard practice to provide a family tree of, for example, Cadmus' family when teaching the *Bacchae* or the Julio-Claudians when teaching Ancient

History or Tacitus' *Annals*. But this could also be used to help students recognise characters in a language textbook to aid comprehension and retention of the storyline. For example, the characters could be shown in colour-coded groups according to their family relationships or status to highlight the connections. Students can sound out the names to become familiar with their pronunciation and discuss what the groupings might suggest about the relationships between the characters. The character map can also be used for later revision to recall who is who and it could lead to further discussion of what students have learned about the lives of these characters.

## Explaining and modelling

In *Making Every Lesson Count* (2015), Shaun Allison and Andy Tharby define three principles that are at the heart of effective explanations:

1 They should be tethered to something students already know about.
2 They should allow for the limited capacity of the human memory.
3 They should aim to transform abstract ideas into concrete ones.

The explanation should be simple enough to understand but also be credible and clearly defined so the students understand the parameters of the concept and believe it to be true. Where possible, make students curious about the concept and engage them through storytelling. This will probably be easier with Classical Civilisation and Ancient History lessons than with teaching language – it is hard to tell a story about the subjunctive. However, the story should not be so captivating that the students only remember the story, not the intended learning behind it. It is also important to think ahead to any potential misconceptions so these can hopefully be avoided or quickly identified through questioning.

Questions for teachers and departments to ask when planning how they will explain a new topic or content point include:

- What prior learning does this link to?
- What is the bigger picture that it fits into?
- Should I start with the bigger picture or the small?
- What order should instruction be given in?
- What pieces of information will students have to link together to be able to understand it?
- How can I break down this content into steps?
- What skills will they need to be able to implement it?

- What should be the ratio between time spent on instruction, modelling and practice (whole class, group, individual)?
- How can they practise using it?
- How will I know they have understood it?
- How will I know they have learned it?

Modelling plays a powerful role in the classroom, as we learn by copying others, by observing how something is done and then trying it out for ourselves. Rosenshine's fourth principle was to provide models as a way to reduce the cognitive load of a task and make problem solving faster (2012). Moreover, modelling of problem-solving and learning strategies helps develop self-regulation and self-efficacy (Schunk, 1981; Zimmerman, 1989). However, just watching someone complete a task is not enough. The person modelling needs to be explicit in how and what they are modelling, so the learner can analyse, interpret and recall what is happening and how it was done (Hattie and Yates, 2013). The modelling should also be done in steps, so the learner has time to process the steps taken.

### Live modelling

Live modelling allows students to observe your thought processes and the strategies you use while completing a task. It also gives them the opportunity to ask questions and for you to check their understanding as you go along. It is particularly useful for modelling writing techniques (Allison and Tharby, 2015) and not only shows students how to do something well but also how to cope with, and move on from, any mistakes. Live modelling is made much easier and quicker when done digitally, using a computer and projector or a visualiser, but it can also be done by writing on the board.

In the Classics classroom, live modelling could be used to show students how to write a particular part of an essay, for example, how to write a PEEL (Point, Evidence, Explanation, Link) paragraph, integrate secondary scholarship or develop literary analysis of a text. It could also be used to model how to translate sentences, parts of stories or particular grammar points.

### Model answers

A model answer can also be prepared in advance and analysed by the class to determine what a successful piece of work looks like (sometimes known as WAGOLL, 'what a good one looks like'). A model answer could be given either before a task, so students know the ideal form they are aiming for, or as feedback, so students can compare their work with the model. However, although model answers are an effective form of feedback for improving performance, they should be used alongside, and not instead of, personalised feedback (Huxham, 2007).

Non-examples which include elements that do not meet the assessment requirements can also be used alongside model answers to help learners distinguish between standards of work. An example for GCSE Greek is given below.

## Non-example model answer activity – GCSE Greek 8-mark question

In this passage, how does Herodotus show that Mycerinus thought his fate was unjust?

In your answer you may wish to consider:

- Mycerinus' reaction to the oracle's message
- the nature of Mycerinus' response to the oracle.

You must refer to the Greek and discuss Herodotus' use of language. [8 marks]

Rewrite these exemplar paragraphs to suggest how they could be improved to better meet the requirements of the assessment objectives.

| Exemplar version | My version |
|---|---|
| Herodotus shows his fate was unjust as he was going to die soon. The shortness of his life is shown by the reference to the numbers six and seven. | |
| Mycerinus' displeasure at his fate is shown by the phrase 'δεινὸν ποιησάμενος'. | |
| Mycerinus went as far as to rebuke the gods 'ἔπεμψεν … τῷ θεῷ ὀνείδισμα' emphasising how he felt. | |
| The alliteration of 'πατὴρ' and 'πάτρως' makes his point stand out. | |
| Mycerinus lists all the terrible things his father and uncle did to show how unfair he thought their actions were. They 'ἀποκλείσαντες… μεμνημένοι… φθείροντες'. | |
| He uses the pronoun 'I' to show how he does not deserve this fate. | |

Care must be taken when using non-examples to ensure that all students are clear as to which parts need improvement and how this could be achieved, so that misconceptions are not learned and reproduced later.

## Worked examples

To complete a task successfully, students have to acquire 'the procedural knowledge of *what* actions to perform and *how* to perform them and the conceptual knowledge of *why* to perform those actions' (van Gog et al., 2019, p. 183). Worked examples are therefore an effective way of helping novices develop skills, as they model what success looks like (Hattie and Yates, 2013) and require learners to focus on the specific steps of the task.

Worked examples are predominantly used in STEM subjects but can be used in any area to help students learn how to solve problems. We do this in Latin and Greek when we give example sentence translations for new grammatical constructions and then ask students to translate similar ones themselves. In Classical Civilisation and Ancient History, they can be used for practising how to answer short-answer questions, how to develop introductions or conclusions or how to engage with secondary scholarship.

Worked examples have been shown to be a particularly successful strategy when followed by a practice example (van Gog et al., 2019). This format helps students to maintain their focus and motivation in completing the tasks and also helps the teacher identify any misconceptions early on (Lovell, 2020). For example, the following exercise adapts a worked example format taken from Lovell to develop literary analysis skills at GCSE.

# Worked example task – GCSE Latin literature 6-mark question

What makes Juvenal's description of Umbricius' journey through Rome an effective piece of writing? [6 marks]

Use the worked examples as a template to answer the practice exercises.

| | Worked example | Practice exercise |
|---|---|---|
| 1 | *arto vicorum in flexu* (lines 3–4)<br>Find an example of hyperbaton and explain its effect.<br><br>The separation of the adjective *arto* (narrow) from its noun *flexu* (winding) and the resulting jumbling of the word order in this line mimics the twisting of the narrow streets to reinforce how winding they are. | *magno populus premit agmine* (line 11)<br>Find an example of hyperbaton and explain its effect.<br><br>The separation of … |
| 2 | *leget aut scribet vel dormiet* (line 8)<br>Explain the effect of the tricolon.<br><br>The tricolon of *leget*, *scribet* and *dormiet* (he reads, writes and sleeps) reinforces that there were many things that the rich man could do in his litter and that travelling for him was a useful activity. The fact that he could write or even sleep inside highlights how comfortable the ride must have been. | *ferit hic cubito, ferit assere duro alter, at hic tignum capiti incutit, ille metretam* (lines 12–13)<br><br>The listing of … |
| 3 | *calcor* (line 15)<br>Explain the effect of the passive mood.<br><br>The passive form *calcor* (I am trodden on) suggests that Umbricius has no agency here and he can do nothing to stop people treading on him. | *vehetur* (line 6)<br>Explain the effect of the passive mood.<br><br>The passive form … |

Worked examples also offer opportunities for self-explanation, which encourages students to discuss the principles underlying the worked example, leading to deeper metacognitive understanding and greater transfer of information to long-term memory. They also provide teachers with additional feedback on whether students have grasped the content. For example, this exercise, also adapted from Lovell (2020), could be used for language learning.

### Worked example exercise – KS3 Latin

Discuss with your partner the answer to the explanation questions. How did Claudia know to choose these verbs to complete the sentences?

| Worked example | Explanation |
| --- | --- |
| Claudia was practising how to form verbs in Latin. She answered these questions as follows.<br><br>*Complete the sentences with the correct form of the verb:*<br>1  ego in foro <u>laboro</u>.<br>2  tu in cella <u>dormis</u>.<br>3  Lucius in popina <u>est</u>. | Sentence 1: How did Claudia know to use '*laboro*' in the first sentence?<br><br>Sentence 2: How did Claudia know to use '*dormis*' in the second sentence?<br><br>Sentence 3: How did Claudia know to use '*est*' in the third sentence? |

#### Faded examples

Worked examples work best with novices and should be replaced by independent problem solving once learners become familiar with a skill. Faded examples are therefore one way to graduate learners through guided practice towards independent practice. They can be used with language learning to focus students on a particular grammar point, as shown below with practice of the agent and instrument with passive verbs:

### Faded example exercise – GCSE Latin language

Work through the task to complete or translate all the sentences. Use the worked examples to help you.

1  senex **a pueris** salutabatur. The old man was being greeted **by the children**.

2  miles **gladio** necabatur. The soldier was being killed **by a sword**.

3  naves **tempestate** delebantur. The ships were being destroyed **by a** _____ .

4  **a servo** adiuvabar. I was being helped **by the** _____ .

5  pompa **a rege** spectabatur.

6  **a feminis saxis** oppugnabamur.

7  cur a nauta adiuvabaris?

8  bestiae ab arena a gladiatoriis agebantur.

Faded examples could also be used to develop essay-writing skills, particularly at GCSE. The following example uses a faded model answer to introduce students to 8-mark questions in GCSE Greek. The same format could be used with Latin, Classical Civilisation or Ancient History students.

## Faded example – GCSE Greek literature 8-mark question

1  Read through the first paragraph as an example.

2  Fill in the gaps using the words in the box below to complete the second paragraph.

3  Write two more paragraphs to complete the answer to the question.

**How does Herodotus engage the audience in lines 1–5 of Psammetichus? [8 marks]**

Herodotus engages the audience straight away by stressing the supposed antiquity of the Egyptians. They thought that they were 'πρώτους γενέσθαι πάντων ἀνθρώπων' (the first of all men). The word πρώτους is repeated throughout the passage (πρῶτοι, προτέρους) to bring the audience's focus to this important question of who were the first men. The word πάντων also suggests that this search is universal and the Egyptians were comparing themselves favourably to the whole world. Herodotus also mentions the name of Psammetichus _____ in the first sentence and the _____ of the _____ βασιλεῦσαι and βασιλεύσας meaning 'to be king' highlight his _____ and _____ . This _____ the audience in the story, as they would want to _____ more about this Egyptian _____ who they may or may not have heard of before.

| repetition | status | engages | king |
| learn | twice | importance | verbs |

55

## Scaffolds

A scaffold provides a temporary support for learning to help students develop their skills and confidence when undertaking a new task. Scaffolding is recommended by the Educational Endowment Foundation (EEF) for use with students with SEND (EEF, 2021) but again is beneficial for the whole class as scaffolds help to reduce frustration over completing a task, allow teachers to maintain high expectations, and guide students to becoming independent learners. However, overreliance on scaffolds can have a negative effect and so we must carefully consider the type of scaffold to use, as well as when to introduce and remove it so its use does not impede the development of independent learning.

**Link:** 'Special educational needs in mainstream schools' (https://educationendowmentfoundation.org.uk/education-evidence/guidance-reports/send)

Scaffolds can be visual, verbal or written. They include repeating words to demonstrate pronunciation, thinking aloud, pre-teaching vocabulary, providing sentence starters or worked examples, and using live modelling or graphic organisers, many of which have already been discussed.

### Essay planning

Understanding the requirements for each type of exam question can prove challenging. Students are often unsure how to approach a question and how to format their answers. Moreover, they need to be taught how to write a concise answer in timed conditions that addresses the assessment objectives, showing relevant knowledge and developing a perceptive interpretation and analysis of the material. The combined use of model answers, live modelling, essay proformas and writing frames are powerful tools to develop these skills. Below are examples of different styles of essay-writing scaffolds in Classics.

## Essay planning grid – Eduqas GCSE Latin literature 16-mark question

'The Romans saw love as a difficult and painful emotion.' To what extent do you agree with this view?

In your answer you should:

- present a balanced and logical argument;
- support your argument with at least four examples (in English) from the passages and pictures you have studied;
- write in continuous prose without bullet points. [16 marks]

Complete the table with points from the text that you could use to answer the question under these headings (there is space for you also to add your own). Then explain and develop each point to show how it answers the question.

|  | Point | Evidence from the texts | Explanation and development |
|---|---|---|---|
| **Agree** | Heartbreak | • Catullus felt wretched after breaking up with Lesbia.<br>• List of questions asking her about how she will now be alone. | • Strength of his emotion and his attempts to force himself to be strong show the pain of his heartbreak.<br>• His bitterness is clear as he imagines her being alone and suffering. |
|  | Unrequited love |  |  |
|  | Marital problems |  |  |
|  | Conflicting emotions |  |  |
|  | Pain of seeing loved one suffer |  |  |
|  |  |  |  |
|  |  |  |  |
| **Disagree** | Love in marriage |  |  |
|  | Joy of kisses |  |  |
|  |  |  |  |
|  |  |  |  |

## Writing frame – A-level Classical Civilisation 10-mark question

**Explain how Sappho creates an effective representation of Aphrodite's divinity in Poem 1. [10 marks]**

Use these sentence starters to build your answer. Remember to quote from the passage and include points from across the whole of the text given.

- Sappho creates an effective representation of Aphrodite's immortality through …
- Sappho depicts Aphrodite as a regal figure by …
- Sappho suggests that Aphrodite is a goddess who can be called on to help mortals as she …
- Aphrodite is revealed to be a powerful goddess who has power over …
- Aphrodite is presented as a kind and benevolent goddess, as she …
- Sappho depicts Aphrodite as a goddess who you would want on your side, as she …
- The line … shows Aphrodite is …
- Aphrodite's … is illustrated when Sappho says …

## Vocabulary checklist – A-level Ancient History 36-mark question

**How far did Octavian's actions play a role in the breakdown of the Republic? [36 marks]**

Use the vocabulary checklist to help you plan your essay. Try to use as many of these keywords as you can.

| assassination | triumvirate | army | consulship | proscriptions |
| --- | --- | --- | --- | --- |
| Actium | bribery | opposition | veterans | the senate |
| the people | will | triumvir | largesse | Mutina |

# Essay checklist – A-level Latin 15-mark question

Use this checklist to help you write your answer. Read through it before you start, refer to it as you write and then tick off each point at the end if you are happy that you have met the requirement.

| I have ... | |
|---|---|
| given a range of points from across the passage | |
| addressed the specific terms of the question | |
| quoted and translated the Latin I refer to | |
| maintained a coherent line of reasoning throughout | |
| kept my points concise so I can make as many as possible | |
| structured my answer logically | |
| remembered that style supports discussion of content. | |

## Graphic organisers

Learning is a complex process that requires students (and teachers) to grapple with large quantities of interconnected knowledge. David Ausubel's development of the meaningful learning theory proposed that learning and retention of knowledge occur when the learner is able to organise and assimilate new concepts onto a cognitive framework (1963). Graphic organisers present information in a simplified way that can help learners draw out connections and the hierarchy of concepts. They can be used to develop storylines and persuasive arguments, demonstrate concept hierarchies and sequences of knowledge, and bring out the similarities, differences and connections between concepts. They can be adapted for any subject or topic, whether for thematic revision and essay planning or solidifying grammatical knowledge. They can also either be produced by teachers as a learning tool or by students for consolidating knowledge. The examples below can be used across the subject and levels and be easily adapted in content and format to suit your learning intention.

### Example 1: A-level Classical Civilisation
This type of graphic organiser could be given to students with the subsections either completed or blank for them to define their own points. They then annotate the diagram with examples from Sappho's

poems as evidence for each subsection, so encouraging students to recall specific examples to support their points. Students could also produce their own from scratch to revise topics and create essay plans.

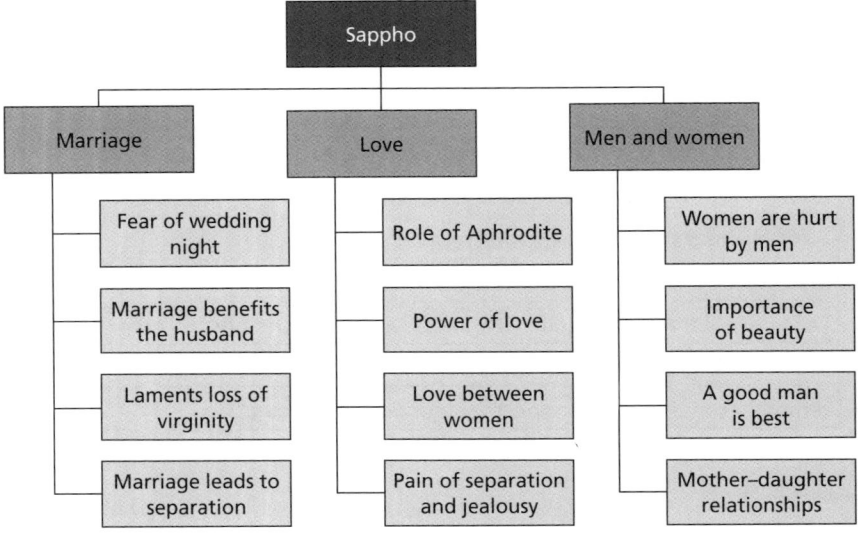

### Example 2: A-level Classical Civilisation

Graphic organisers can clarify sequences of events and timelines. This example was used as a gap-fill starter exercise with students who were struggling to understand the order of prophecies and events that happened before the start of Sophocles' *Oedipus the King*.

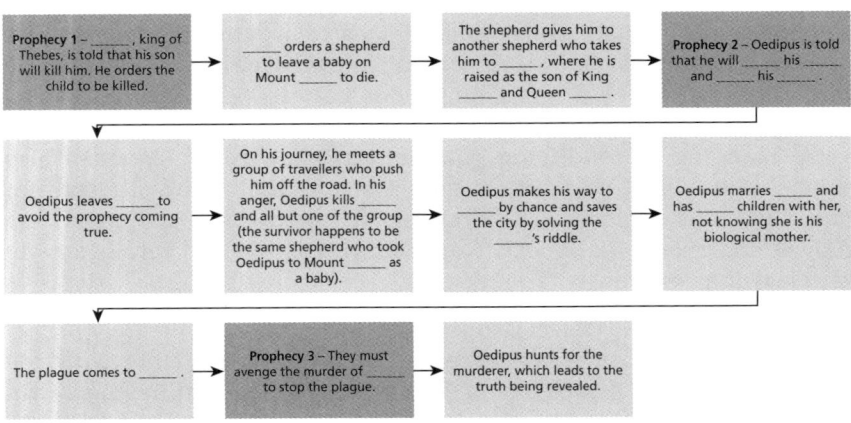

## Example 3: GCSE Latin

The differences between grammatical concepts can also be demonstrated graphically. GCSE students can find it difficult to identify and translate various subjunctive clauses. This diagram helps students identify the differences between constructions that use the subjunctive and enables them to recognise and correctly translate them more easily

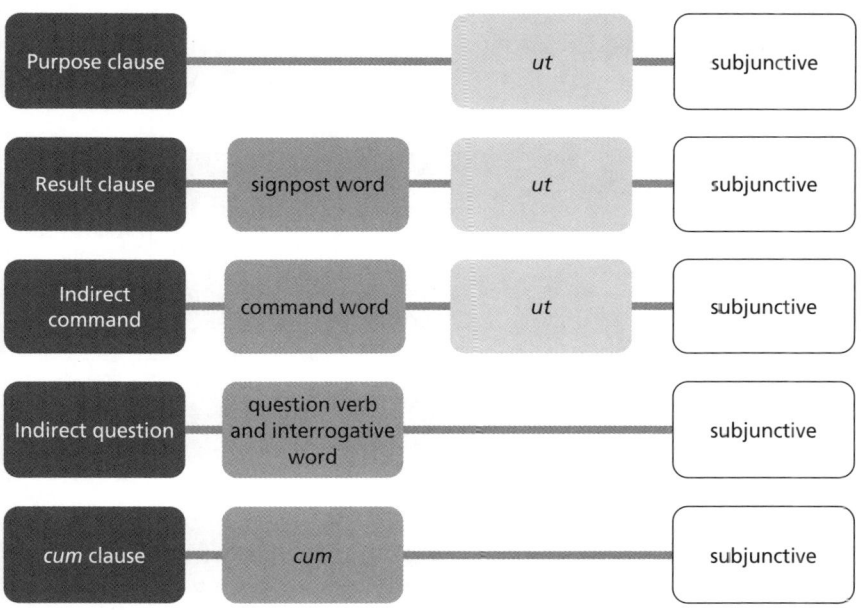

### Example 4: A-level Classical Civilisation or Ancient History

Graphic-organiser templates can also be used by students to develop persuasive writing and essay plans.

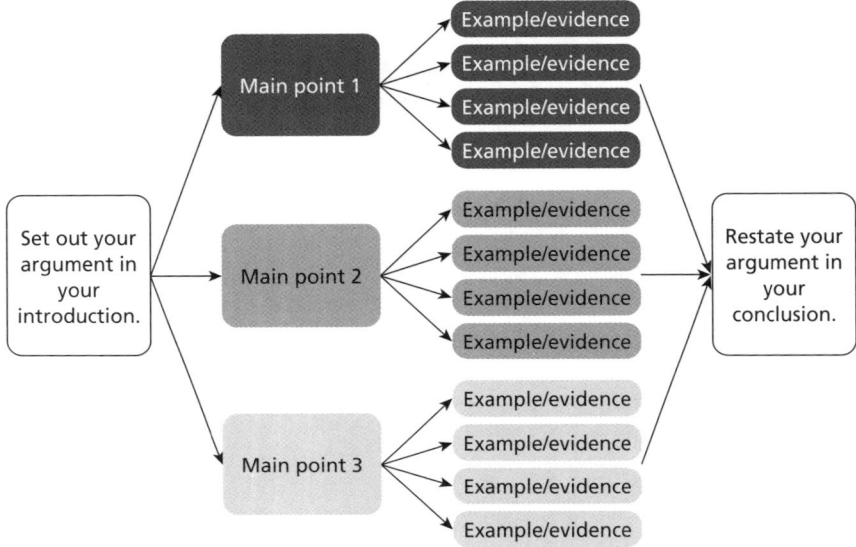

### Concept maps

A concept map is a form of graphic organiser that draws out connections between ideas and concepts and the Generate–Sort–Connect–Elaborate routine can be used to help students create them. This routine asks students to:

- **Generate** – think about this topic and create a list of all ideas and facts that come to mind.
- **Sort** – place the most important ideas in the centre, with more tangential information towards the edges.
- **Connect** – draw lines between points to show connections. Include captions to explain the connection.
- **Elaborate** – add any further ideas that expand on, or add to, your initial ideas.

Students would need sticky notes or small pieces of paper on which to write down their ideas and a piece of A3 paper on which to arrange their points.

**Link:** 'Generate–Sort–Connect–Elaborate' (https://pz.harvard.edu/sites/default/files/Generate-Sort-Connect-Elaborate_0.pdf)

Concept maps can also be used to breakdown complex grammatical concepts such as the gerund.

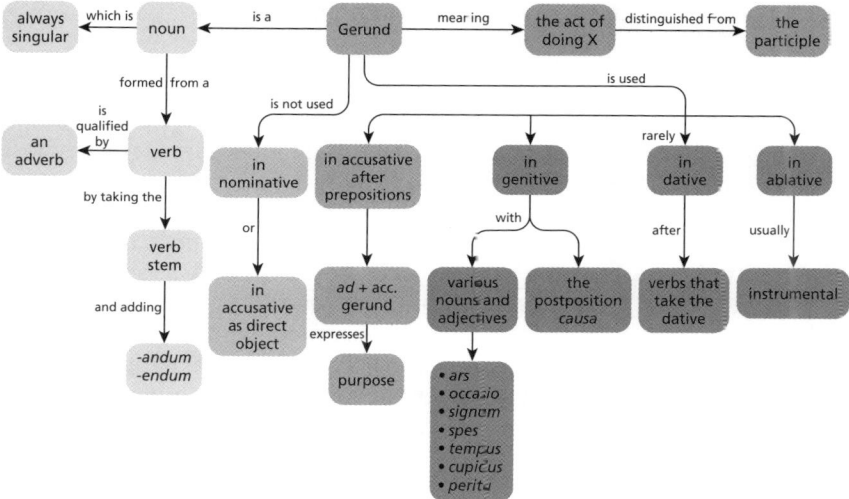

## Practice tasks

The I/We/You approach is a simple learning model that moves from modelling to guided practice and then independent practice. However, the pressures of limited curriculum time for many classical subjects, particularly for those taught off-timetable, means that these important stages of practice can be neglected. Rosenshine found that when teachers used guided practice their students were more engaged in independent work and had fewer misconceptions (2012). Students 'learn what they do' (Nuthall, 2007, p. 36), so the quality of the practice they undertake directly correlates with the quality of the knowledge they retain and their performance (Allison and Tharby, 2015). Moreover, Nuthall found that students need to meet a piece of information three times before it is learned securely (2007). It is therefore crucial to imbed guided practice into lessons, so that students meet concepts several times and have the opportunity to practise them in order to develop automaticity.

Practice can take the form of simple tasks and short-answer questions to develop fluency of knowledge, such as drills on verb endings, vocabulary or key terminology, which Allison and Tharby call 'practice for fluency' (2015, p. 126). They can also take the form of longer, more challenging tasks that push students outside their comfort zone to develop their wider understanding of a topic. Modelling and scaffolding are also forms of guided practice, as it is through practice that Rosenshine's principles overlap and reinforce each other (Sherrington, 2019).

Another of Rosenshine's principles (2012) states that practice tasks should be designed so that students can obtain an 80% success rate – a task should not be so hard that they are practising errors, but there should still be a desired level of challenge. He found this success was most evident when teachers introduced material in small steps and prepared students more thoroughly for independent practice. To help ensure a high success rate, the teacher should circulate to check for misconceptions, give feedback and re-teach where necessary. Students should also be encouraged to ask questions when they are stuck and to reflect on their progress and outcomes. As students become more confident in the skills and knowledge being practised, any scaffolds and teacher support should be gradually removed so that students come to rely only on their own resources to complete the task and motivate themselves to achieve the learning goal.

Many examples of practice activities have already been given in the modelling and scaffolding sections, so they are not repeated here. Some additional activities are listed below.

### Fold it in

This is an idea taken from *Making Every Lesson Count* and serves to provide a 'useful conduit through which students move back and forth between ideas and concepts, tacitly practising them as they go' (Allison and Tharby, 2015, p. 141). It helps teachers develop a scheme of work that embeds practice of key ideas and concepts throughout a topic or unit. For the A-level Ancient History Julio-Claudians module this might look like this example:

1. Define the key concepts and themes of the topic as given in the specification:
   - constitutional power
   - administration of Rome
   - relationship to the Senate

- relationship to the army
- relationship to the people
- religion
- imperial family
- challenges to their reign.

2 Introduce students to these concepts and themes and the ideal of how they were expected to work in the Republic.

3 Use these concepts and themes as a framework through which to explore the nature of the reigns of the emperors.

4 As the course progresses, students are able to identify, analyse and compare evidence on these key concepts and themes with less guidance from the teacher.

5 At the end of the unit, students are able to draw out evidence from the sources to compare and contrast these themes across all five emperors.

## Peer essay development

This is an extended version of think–pair–share to develop essay-writing skills and build a whole-class sample essay plan.

1 Students are given an essay title and asked to 'Blurt it out' to see what they know about this topic.

2 Students work in pairs to identify the key points that run through their notes.

3 The teacher calls on students to read out their most promising points and writes these on the board.

4 The class decides on the best points which are to form the basis of the whole-class essay plan.

5 Each pair writes a paragraph answer for one or two points from the whole-class plan.

6 Each pair reads out the answer they wrote for their point. These can also be displayed on the board with a visualiser or other device.

7 Students write their own answers to the essay question.

## Feedback

Feedback is an essential tool that teachers use to develop student understanding and improve their performance. But what makes it effective? Strong formative feedback gives students information about the correct results, some explanation and a specific activity to undertake to move them forward (Wiliam, 2017). This feedback may take any format, such as WWW ('What went well') and EBI ('Even better if') or a simple tick for what went well and an arrow for targets to improve. But to ensure that students engage with the feedback, a task should be included that requires them to demonstrate their understanding of what needs to be improved and how this can be done. For Latin and Greek, this might be translating further example sentences to practise a particular tense. For Classical Civilisation and Ancient History, it might be rewriting a paragraph to develop their use of sources in an essay.

Hattie and Timperley (2007) identified three feedback questions that help the teacher and student to assess a student's understanding of the feedback and improvement tasks.

1. *Where am I going?* To understand how the learning goals can be attained, which they termed the now common phrase 'success criteria'.
2. *How am I going?* To assess how the student did relative to a task or performance goal, which they termed 'feed-back dimension'.
3. *Where to next?* To provide guidance on what strategies, processes and tasks can be used to lead to greater learning.

Whole-class feedback can be used to save the teacher time writing lengthy comments on all students' work and puts the onus on students to relate the feedback to their own work and answer these three questions. Whole-class feedback for a KS3 Latin class that has completed a homework task on the dative might look like the following example.

### Whole class feedback – KS3 Latin

**What went well:**
- Vocabulary
- Looking at verb endings to identify who is doing the action
- Identifying and translating the dative – to/for

**Common errors:**
- *tradidit* = handed over
- *nolebat* = did not want, refused
- *volo* = I want
- *appropinquabamus* = we were approaching
- *rem gravem* = a serious matter
- *liberi laetissimi* = the very happy children

**Do next tasks:**
1. Do your corrections.
2. Translate these sentences into English. All contain a dative.
   a. senes laetissimi foro appropinquabant.
   b. puella matri pecuniam tradidit.
   c. miles imperatori nuntium narravit.

**Summary:**
Write a summary comment explaining what went well in your work (did you do what you set out to achieve?) and what you should think about or do next time you answer a similar task to improve on your errors.

Students are likely to make similar errors to each other, so a key can be used to indicate which areas they did well in and where they need to focus on for improvement. The table below suggests comments that might be used for a GCSE language paper. The teacher writes the corresponding letters on the front of students' exam papers and students must then read and engage with the specific feedback to highlight on their reflection sheets what went well and what they need to improve before completing their own reflection and feedback tasks.

| What went well | Areas to improve |
| --- | --- |
| A – Vocabulary | A – Vocabulary |
| B – Singular and plural | B – Singular and plural |
| C – Tenses | C – Tenses |
| D – Look at the lemma (part of passage quoted) | D – Look at the lemma (part of passage quoted) |
| E – Comparatives and superlatives | E – Comparatives and superlatives |
| F – Sentence structure | F – Sentence structure |
| G – Grammar questions | G – Grammar questions |

## Daily, weekly and monthly review

Rosenshine's final principle (2012) is to review material weekly and monthly, which can be done through quizzing, questioning, correcting homework or asking students to identify points of difficulty. This extensive practice allows students to develop well-connected schemata that integrate prior and new content, address misconceptions before they embed, identify gaps in knowledge and improve the automaticity of knowledge retrieval from long-term memory. As such, it helps move the novice towards becoming an expert.

One review method uses retrieval practice, which puts the onus on students to recall prior knowledge from long-term memory into the working memory. It can be as simple as asking students to write down two or three things they remember from last lesson or a previous topic. Retrieval has become increasingly popular in recent years and is shown to be effective in many subject areas, including language and vocabulary learning (Karpicke and Roediger, 2008). Retrieval practice can particularly benefit vocabulary learning when used alongside corrective feedback (Li et al., 2024). However, there remains debate about how effective retrieval practice is for learning vocabulary and grammar, both of which are more difficult to revise generatively.

Kate Jones (2019, pp. 42–43) proposes that for retrieval practice to be effective it needs to:

- involve everyone
- specify the knowledge that will be tested
- be varied
- be easy to check and correct
- be generative
- be time efficient
- be workload efficient.

Retrieval tasks have the most effect when they include a mix of both fact-based retrieval and higher-order retrieval (Agarwal and Bain, 2019). Furthermore, retrieval should be low stakes; marks should not be collected from retrieval tasks, so that students focus on accurately retrieving and understanding content rather than achieving a particular score.

**Links:** 'Why daily, weekly and monthly reviews matter' (www.innerdrive.co.uk/blog/reviews-matter/)

'Unleash the science of learning' (www.retrievalpractice.org/)

Sarah Elliot explains how and why she uses retrieval practice for GCSE Classical Civilisation.

## Case study of retrieval practice in Classical Civilisation
### Sarah Elliot, Streatham and Clapham High School

I was introduced to the term 'retrieval practice' a couple of years ago. I had always thought reviewing past learning in a lesson was important to ensure students could link the new material to previously met material, but I have now made it a standard practice for my lessons.

When Bradley Busch from Inner Drive came to school last year for our January INSET, he enumerated a number of advantages of retrieval practice as a standard element of every lesson, based on Roediger and Karpicke's 2006 paper:

- Retrieval practice creates connections between new and existing knowledge.
- It strengthens memory traces and ensures that memory is 'robust under pressure'.
- It means that the key information is more likely to move from working memory to long-term memory.
- And then there's the 'Matthew effect' – the more you know, the easier it is to know more.

So how have I been using it for Classical Civilisation?

1 **Socrative quizzes.** Ben Tanner, in an excellent Keynote Educational course on the new (at the time) GCSE syllabus, introduced me to Socrative, which is fantastic for quizzes. You can choose multiple-choice, true/false and short-answer options and it marks the first two types for you (bonus for teacher workload) and then I manually mark the short-answer options. I do this at random, unexpected points in the GCSE course and occasionally with notice given and revision time scheduled, and the students seem to love it. I keep it low-stakes – there's no pass mark and no preparation needed most of the time, so students don't get anxious and quite enjoy the challenge.

2 **The walking chocolate bar.** I picked up the idea of the walking chocolate bar, which is a type of collaborative brain dump, at an Optimus More Able

conference. You take a piece of paper (I use brown to add to the idea of 'chocolate') and fold it into eight segments. Each student writes as much as they can remember in the first segment. They then walk round the classroom to give it to a second student to write down different information in the second segment. And so on, until all eight segments are filled in. Once you get to the eighth student, you tell them to check earlier info and correct any mistakes. I then take in all sheets, look through them to check for misconceptions/inaccuracies and award stickers to the eight students who contributed to the best sheet. An example is shared through the QR codes below.

3 **Big Post-its®.** Aisha Khan-Evans, who leads the Latin with Classics PGCE at King's College London, introduced me to the use of Post-its in teaching. Because students aren't writing 'in neat' in their exercise books, they feel more comfortable with writing on something less permanent. I like to get the really big Post-its and use them over a series of lessons – this way they can see progress too. The 'last lesson, last week, last month' approach works well, as do brain dumps or even simple verbal Q and As, where students write down the answer. They could even be used as mini-whiteboards, so that the teacher can check for understanding.

Further examples of retrieval questions for Homer's *Iliad* and a spider diagram comparing Pandora and Helen are also available through the QR codes.

**Links:** Socrative (www.socrative.com)

### Blurt it out (brain dumps)

This is a very simple retrieval task that takes no preparation time. Give students a topic area (for example, the character of Odysseus, Alexander the Great's control over Greece, Herodotus' depiction of the Egyptians, uses of subjunctive) and ask them to write down as much as they can remember in a set time. Depending on the topic, they could also be asked to create a visual representation which requires greater engagement with the information, as the students have to decide how to transfer it into a visual form (Enser and Enser, 2020). The class can then share what they remembered and add to their own notes. This is also an effective revision activity for students to do on their own.

If needed, students could also be given pictures or key words as prompts to help stimulate recall. An example for A-level Classical Civilisation adapted from Kate Jones (2019) is:

A further variation on this is cops and robbers, also adapted from Kate Jones (2019). This task is easy to modify for any topic and is a firm favourite with students. Prompts can also be given if students need additional support.

### Cops and robbers – KS3 Latin

1  Write the title and the following headings in the back of your exercise book.
2  You have four minutes to write as much as you can from memory about Roman baths in the first column.

3  Find someone else in the class to share your answers with. Add any information that they recalled but you didn't in the 'stolen' column.

| My own knowledge | Information I have 'stolen' |
|---|---|
|  |  |

Things to think about:
- rooms in the baths
- activities in the baths
- decoration of the baths
- people in the baths
- atmosphere in the baths.

Retrieval grids

Retrieval grids are another exercise developed from Kate Jones's book (2019) on retrieval. They take more time to prepare but are a great way to review material from a series of lessons or chapters. This format can easily be used with any subject or level.

### Retrieval grid – GCSE Latin language

Answer as many questions as you can. There are 33 points up for grabs in total.

| What are the present tense passive verb endings? | Translate: *audivi hostes fugisse*. | Translate: *his verbis auditis puellae laetissimae erant*. |
|---|---|---|
| What does *portatus* mean? | What is a deponent verb? | What construction does an indirect statement use? |
| How is *ut* translated in a purpose clause? | What is an ablative absolute? | List three prepositions that take the ablative case. |
| What does *portate* mean? | What do the verbs *scio*, *intellego* and *cognosco* mean? | How is the imperfect subjunctive formed? |

| One point – last lesson | Two points – last week | Three points – 2 weeks ago | Four points – further back |
|---|---|---|---|

## Multiple choice

Multiple-choice questions lack the generative element of retrieval practice but can be used to revise terminology and key details with students who need more scaffolding. However, the challenge in writing multiple-choice questions is in creating alternative options that do not make the correct answer too obvious. Multiple-choice questions can also be made more cognitively challenging by asking students to explain why they chose their answers.

### Multiple-choice questions – KS3 Latin

1  Highlight which translation you think is the correct answer for each sentence.
2  Explain why that answer is correct (and/or why the other answers are incorrect) based on your understanding of Latin noun and verb endings.

| Which translation is correct? | Explain why you chose that answer. |
|---|---|
| What is the meaning of: *amicus currit* <br> A  The friend runs. <br> B  The friends run. | |
| What is the meaning of: *servi dominum salutant* <br> A  The master greets the slave. <br> B  The slave greets the master. <br> C  The slaves greet the master. | |
| What is the meaning of: *canem spectas* <br> A  You see the dog. <br> B  You look at the dog. <br> C  The dog looks at you. | |

### Review of Latin and Greek vocabulary

Generative review tasks, such as blurt it out, work well for topics in Classical Civilisation and Ancient History or for reviewing the content of Latin and Greek set texts. However, they are more difficult to do for language learning, as students need to be provided with more prompts, such as giving them the vocabulary or sentences to translate.

Online testers like Quizlet and Blooket are popular with students and help to engage them in vocabulary revision. Tasks such as 'find the odd one out' or a vocabulary challenge grid can also make vocabulary review more varied. The following example of a vocabulary challenge is used for KS3 Latin, but the same format could easily be adapted for Classical Civilisation and Ancient History terminology.

## Vocabulary challenge – KS3 Latin

Your challenge is to correctly translate enough verbs in the grid to score at least 30 points. The number of points each verb is worth is given at the top of its column.

| 1 point | 2 points | 3 points | 4 points |
|---|---|---|---|
| dormio | habito | saluto | laudo |
| laboro | intro | specto | teneo |
| ambulo | video | festino | possum |
| sum | audio | curro | vendo |

However, reviewing uninflected vocabulary and isolated word forms out of context in artificial lists may not be an effective revision task. In the following case study, Henry Cullen proposes an alternative to the traditional vocabulary test.

## Case study of vocabulary testing by part of speech and including inflected forms
### Henry Cullen, St Albans High School for Girls

How many times have you actually seen the word (and specific form) *porto* appear in a GCSE Latin paper (or 'real Latin' for that matter)? Answer: quite possibly never. Nor, of course, do you see the present tense itself, except for within direct speech.* So it is of limited value, when teaching and testing vocabulary, to test what we never see. Certainly, the word and mental tag *porto* is essential for teacher talk and as the centre of a student's own schema or mental map: 'What verb does this come from?', 'Which Latin word is this English term derived from?', 'Which verb does this [other verb] go like?' and so on. But when it comes to testing vocabulary, it is much more useful – and more mentally stretching – to test inflected forms, link the Latin to derivatives, and test words in the context of mini-sentences.

It is also hugely helpful, I have found, to teach and test vocab by part of speech, particularly in Year 10 of a GCSE course. Hence, I don't ask students at first just to revise page 1 of the vocab list, with its jumble of parts of speech – instead, I save this for revision in Year 11. Rather, in Year 10 I ask students to revise all the first conjugation verbs in the vocab list, and then work through all the other types of word in sequence. This can easily be done over one or two terms and provides an opportunity to consolidate the grammar along the way. It helps to issue vocab lists sorted into part of speech and to flag, explicitly, the endings which will be seen with each conjugation/declension.

Then I design tests in such a way that they test in different ways and aim to stretch, as well as preparing students for the moment they actually see these forms 'in the wild' of a translation passage: thus I don't just test *porto*, *nuntio*, etc. but rather *portavisti*, *portare*, *portabit*, *nuntia*, *nuntiatus est* and so on, too. Moreover, if possible, I include grammar questions about the part of speech being covered and short sentences involving examples of the part of speech being revised (even if they can sound silly or contrived) – the vocab item is thus seen in the context of a short sentence, rather than isolated on a page. An example vocabulary test is shared through the QR code below.

All of this serves to make vocab revision and testing a more cognitively engaging process, since it reinforces the possible permutations of vocab stems and person/case endings that a student might actually see. It confronts head-on what can often be seen as cognitively hardest about Latin – the problem that recognising the first bit of a word (the root '*port-*' for example) is only half the battle, since it is only by making sense of the ending too that you can properly relate the Latin word to the others around it in the sentence. Word endings matter and they make an inflected language like Latin much more sophisticated and complex than we are used to as speakers of modern English, but the more they can be encountered and practised, including in vocab tests, the less scary and arbitrary they seem.

* So what do you *actually* see most frequently in GCSE-style passages? Some years ago I made a word cloud based on the first 50 passages in the first edition of *Latin Stories*, and the PDF available through the following QR code was the result. Note the frequency of 'little words' like pronouns and the complete absence of first person present active indicatives.

As Henry Cullen discusses in his case study, there is benefit in asking students to translate whole sentences, as retrieval has a stronger effect when there is a close match between the format of the retrieval practice and the format of the final examination (Yang et al., 2021). For example, instead of giving students a list of words to translate, task them with translating sentences that only include words from the vocabulary they have been set to learn that week or within a chapter.

The example exercise below is based on vocabulary from the Eduqas GCSE vocabulary list, which was reorganised into 18 subsections according to word type before being given to students. These words come from section one, first declension nouns and first conjugation verbs.

### Vocabulary retrieval sentences – GCSE Latin

You have four minutes to translate as many of these sentences as you can into English. Once the time is up, you will have two minutes to work with your partner to check your translations and, between you, produce your best translations of all five.

1  nauta ianuam oppugnat.
2  ad silvam festinare conor.
3  meam vitam amo.
4  filia dominam adiuvat.
5  ancilla pecuniam celat.

Sentences that focus on a specific grammar point also work well as a review task, but if the focus of the retrieval task is to practise a grammar point, either the vocabulary used should be familiar to students or a vocabulary list should be provided, so that students' cognitive focus is on the grammar point, rather than identifying unfamiliar vocabulary. Further support could be provided in the form of options from which to choose their answers or by giving students access to grammar tables while they complete the task.

### Review of Latin and Greek literature

Review of GCSE and A-level set texts is made up of three distinct elements: the translation and meaning of the text, the author's choice and use of language, and the themes present in the text. As the thematic essays are written solely in English, revision of the themes of the set texts can be done with no prompts, using quizzing, blurt it out, retrieval grids, etc. However, to review the translation and use of language within the texts, students need to be provided with the relevant passages from which to work. There are various tasks that can be used to reflect the format of what students are required to do in the examination: translation, comprehension questions, identifying and translating phrases from the passage, and identifying language or style points. Variety and regular spaced review are vital for students to maintain a solid recall and understanding of all the set texts. Examples of retrieval tasks that can be used to recall set texts, through quizzing of content, vocabulary and meaning can be accessed through the QR code. In addition to those shown, slides with images related to the content of a source can be used to jog students' memory before completing further retrieval tasks. For example, to revise Horace *Odes* 3.26 'Finished with love', you might include images of a crowbar, temple, locked door, whip and snow, and ask students to explain how they relate to the poem.

In this case study, David Hogg explains how his students create their own personalised revision guide for GCSE Greek set texts throughout the year.

## Case study of teaching literature by creating a revision guide
### David Hogg, Kelmscott School

I think that it is very important that students take ownership of a set text, as this not only demystifies it but also creates affinity for the words. To this end, I prepare a literature guide, full of colour, criticism and imagery which I use to teach the set texts in smaller chunks.

Once a section of the set text has been studied, students are directed to create their personal revision guide. The guide initially follows a format demonstrated using an ex-student's book. However, students can adapt the model to fit their own preferences, as long as it still meets the agreed criteria. Colour, imagery and students' own words and research are vital if the revision booklet moves past a 'task for the teacher' and instead becomes a useful revision tool.

Once students understand what their revision guide should look like and they have settled on their method of working, they find the task of completing it after studying a section of the literature a useful decompression task – it is a chance for them to get their ideas in order and 'think slowly' about the section. In the run-up to exams, students refer to these books and, because of their formatting, students don't need to revise with other Classics students, as answers in the guide are in English, so anyone can help test them.

Students make a revision section for each corresponding section of the literature booklet they have been provided with and lessons follow a routine pattern – around 10 lines of the set text are studied and then students complete the guide for that section. Thus, they do it a little bit at a time.

There are six directed sections:

1. Greek text with word order indicated
2. a translation of the Greek text
3. an image that sums up that section using colour and quotations from the text for dual-coding purposes
4. student summary of the section
5. GCSE-style questions using the stems from OCR exams papers with a mark for each question
6. context or wider knowledge, where students carry out their own research into any character, theme, reference, social or historical context that has emerged in that section.

These sections allow the guide to become an active document rather than a passive one. Examples of the format are provided through the QR codes.

Performing the task of creating the revision guide builds confidence as students move from being passive viewers of a text to actively owning it.

## What does Mode B look like in Classics teaching?

We have so far discussed what Tom Sherrington coined Mode A teaching: the teacher-led instruction that is the bread and butter of the classroom and which develops students' knowledge, skills and understanding to prepare them for assessments and examinations. Mode B teaching in comparison is the tasks that spark awe and allow students to explore and discover the wonders of the ancient world. Matthew Routledge, who was Head of Department in one of the first schools that author Jessica Dixon taught in, called this 'Classics joy' and it encompasses all the myriad ways in which we can inspire our students to love our subject(s). This Mode B teaching is a vital part of our teaching practice, as intrinsic motivation and enjoyment of a subject are important predictors for academic achievement (Taylor et al., 2014) and enjoyment of a subject is an important factor in option choices (Fisher, 2001).

Mode B includes going off-piste to tell a story about mythology, using role play and drama to explore a character or story, enquiry projects, and visiting museums and archaeological sites. These tasks should give students the opportunity for choice, a key element in developing a sense of autonomy and improving motivation (Ryan and Deci, 2020).

## Projects

For schools in which Latin is compulsory for all or parts of KS3, there will come a time when summer examinations are over and students who have already decided that they are dropping Latin become increasingly demotivated. This happens in Dixon's school at the end of Year 8 and is exacerbated by the fact that the KS3 examinations are held before May half term, leaving students who are dropping the subject with less incentive to learn Latin for the second half of the summer term. In Dixon's school, which is an all-girls school, this is counteracted through a project called 'The Super Women of the Ancient World'. The key to this project, and the reason students buy into it so readily, is the high level of choice and creativity that they are given, which builds a sense of control and autonomy. Students are provided with suggestions of historical and mythological ancient women for research, such as Hypatia, Circe, Eumachia, female gladiators and the Amazons, and are given guidance on where they can find suitable online resources, but they are free to choose their own subject. After setting the task parameters and the success criteria by which their work will be assessed, students are given free rein to present their work however they desire. Every year students produce incredibly creative responses, including plays, films, stop-animation, artwork, biographies, interpretative dances, Instagram accounts and news broadcasts. It is an incredibly positive and rewarding way to end the year and hopefully inspires those who will no longer be taking Latin to continue being curious about the ancient world.

Project work can be just as beneficial for students in KS4 and KS5. Francesca Grilli explains how projects have been incorporated into the A-level Classical Civilisation scheme of work at Runshaw College.

## Case study of enquiry-based project work in A-level Classical Civilisation

### Francesca Grilli, Runshaw College

In March 2020, our students were sent home during the pandemic and we noticed many were struggling with motivation and missing deadlines. We therefore decided to pivot towards more enquiry- and project-based tasks that offered our students the opportunity to incorporate their own strengths and areas of interest. We received such positive feedback, and the quality of the final work was so impressive, that we decided to keep it in our scheme of learning once we returned to classroom teaching.

Our creative project is centred on the women of Homer's *Odyssey* and is introduced to students mid-way through the year once they have covered a substantial amount of the text. It begins with some preliminary tasks to aid recall of the female characters, such as a speed-dating task, and then we aid students with the research element of the task by providing a list of suitable *Omnibus* articles, Massolit lectures and podcasts to choose from. They are encouraged to record the name of the scholar and their key ideas in a document as they go and this in turn helps with the scholarship requirement of the A-level Classical Civilisation specification.

The end format is entirely up to the individual student and they are given the Easter holidays to complete it. Over the years we have received a broad variety of submissions, including Greek vases, plays and even embroidery inspired by the women of the *Odyssey*. We do stipulate, however, that if the final project is a piece of artwork, students must also submit an accompanying description of the represented ideas. Students all receive individual feedback based on assessment criteria such as their engagement with scholars and ability to cite specific supporting evidence from Homer. This then feeds into a timed 30-mark essay on women in the *Odyssey*, which we complete in class the week after they have submitted the project.

As we have our classroom grouped by teams such as the Greeks, Romans and Persians, we also added a competitive element to the task and awarded first, second and third prizes. The winners, and any highly commended entries, also receive the ultimate form of *kleos* in that they feature on the Runshaw Classics Instagram account.

For examples of the many entries we have received over the years, please see our social media pages @runshawclassics.

## Flipped learning

Flipped learning or a flipped classroom have become increasingly popular teaching methods in recent years. The formal pedagogical approach of Flipped Learning is defined by the Flipped Learning Network (2014) as one 'in which direct instruction moves from the group learning space to the individual learning space, and the resulting group space is transformed into a dynamic, interactive learning environment where the educator guides students as they apply concepts and engage creatively in the subject matter.' It must also be based on four pillars:

1 Flexible environment – teachers provide a flexible space in which students choose when and where they learn.
2 Learning culture – learning is learner-centred and made accessible to all through differentiation and feedback.
3 Intentional content – relevant content is created or curated by the teacher to develop conceptual understanding and procedural fluency.
4 Professional educator – teachers are present to provide feedback and use formative assessments to inform future instruction.

**Link:** 'What is Flipped Learning?' (https://flippedlearning.org/wp-content/uploads/2016/07/FLIP_handout_FNL_Web.pdf)

The terms 'flipped learning' (without capitals) or 'flipped classroom' are also used. They refer to a form of blended learning where reading or videos are set for students to prepare in advance of the lesson, so that lesson time can be spent practising tasks, debating key concepts and problem solving. This form is used more in the teaching of Classics.

Students are the driving force of flipped learning and as such it helps to increase student engagement, promotes independent study skills and can lead to a greater understanding of the material studied. As students meet declarative knowledge at their own pace during homework tasks, more classroom time is spent developing and practising procedural knowledge under the supervision of a teacher who can offer feedback and support, rather than students struggling to complete the more difficult conceptual tasks at home on their own. Moreover, it supports the development of autonomy and can be used for exploration outside the curriculum. However, problems can arise if not all students participate in the preparatory learning before the lesson or if the resources provided are not accessible.

Resources for flipped learning can include readings from books and articles, but most often online resources and videos are set for home study. These could be filmed by teachers themselves, but there are many already available on YouTube, TED-Ed or Massolit (a subscription service). There are also many Classics-specific resources, such as Dave Midgley's Stupid Ancient History podcasts, James Renshaw's A-level Ancient History podcasts, and the University of Warwick's bank of online resources organised by subject and key stage. Moreover, sites such as Edpuzzle can make videos more interactive by allowing you to insert questions into the video as students watch it at their own pace.

**Links:** Dave Midgley's Stupid Ancient History podcasts (www.youtube.com/channel/UCamPyE75uCUj3BX-N6Iqf7Q/videos)

The Classics podcast does … (https://classicalassociation.org/the-classics-podcast-does/)

Teaching Resources (STOA) (https://warwick.ac.uk/fac/arts/classics/warwickclassicsnetwork/stoa/)

Edpuzzle (https://edpuzzle.com/)

### A-level Classical Civilisation and Ancient History

Set texts for A-level Classical Civilisation and Ancient History can be taught through a flipped approach. Not only does this reduce time spent on reading the set texts in lessons, it also supports students of all abilities. Lower-ability students benefit from having time to process the texts at their own pace. This allows them to build up their prior knowledge before entering the classroom and as a result they can develop more complex schemata during class discussion and become more confident in discussing the texts in lessons. Higher-ability students are challenged by the opportunity to research further into a topic and by the greater focus given in lessons to debating key concepts and themes and developing analytical skills.

To facilitate this, students should be provided with a pre-reading worksheet to prepare each section of the text (an example is given through the QR code below). Each worksheet should contain the same format and expectations for independent work, so students quickly become used to what is expected of them. This might include:

- retrieval questions on earlier sections of the set text to recall prior knowledge relevant to the next section
- key names or terminology that students have not met before
- key themes linked to the specification
- questions for guided reading (including the line numbers in which the answers can be found)
- identification of key quotations that students feel sum up the themes of the section
- questions for the teacher.

Lessons then start with either a discussion of the retrieval questions from the pre-reading worksheet or a quiz that students answer based on their reading in order to check levels of understanding before the lesson starts. Lesson time is spent talking through the guided reading questions, addressing misconceptions and drawing together the wider themes of the section. Through this approach, it is possible to study the set texts more quickly than reading them through together in class, leaving more time for drawing out comparisons between the sources and for revision of the whole course.

## Competitions

Competitions are an excellent way to boost interest in, and engagement with, classical topics. Many Classics charities run annual competitions, offering prizes ranging from book vouchers to trophies to publication in books. Below is a sample of those available in the year prior to publication.

### Classical Association

#### Poetry

This competition invites aspiring poets either to write an original poem in English that draws inspiration from the ancient world or to translate a poem from an ancient language into English. There are three age categories: Junior (aged 11 and under), Senior (aged 12–18) and Open (aged 19 and above). The first- and second-place winners in each category share a prize fund of £1500 and the poems written by the overall winners of the original and translation categories are narrated by the judges on the CA's Classics podcast.

**Link:** Classical Association Poetry Competition (https://classicalassociation.org/2024-competition/)

### Young Speaker

This competition is aimed at students aged 18–24 and invites them to prepare a presentation in any style (for example, a mini lecture, spoken-word piece, edited short film) on a topic related to the ancient world. The winner delivers their presentation at the Classical Association conference.

**Link:** Classical Association Young Speaker Competition (https://classicalassociation.org/young-speaker-competition/)

### Sam Hood Translation Prize

*Omnibus* magazine awards the annual Sam Hood Translation Prize. It is open to students under 19 who are still in pre-university education. Entrants must write a translation into English from either Greek or Latin prose or verse and are encouraged to make it elegant, stylish and creative. Authors for translation have included Lucian, Euripides, Petronius, Ovid and Sallust. The winning entry wins £75 and a book of classical poetry.

**Link:** Classical Association Sam Hood Translation Prize (https://classicalassociation.org/for-students/essay-and-translation-prizes/)

### Gladstone Memorial Essay Prize

This essay competition is also open to students under 19 and still in full-time education who have not yet completed A-levels, IB or equivalent qualifications. They are asked to write an essay not exceeding 2000 words on a variety of suggested essay titles. Previous titles have included:

- Were the ancient Olympic Games more significant to the ancient Greek world than the modern Olympic Games are to our world today?
- Why does the Trojan War provide such fertile ground for modern retellings? You may discuss more than one modern retelling of a Trojan War story.
- How shocking do you think the poems of either Catullus or Ovid would have been to their ancient audiences?
- Which one piece of artwork (ancient or modern art or sculpture) do you think best captures the telling of a classical myth which you have read? Justify your answer with reference to at least two other pieces of artwork depicting the same myth.

The first prize stands at £200, the second at £100.

**Link:** Classical Association Gladstone Memorial Essay Prize (https://classicalassociation.org/for-students/essay-and-translation-prizes/)

**Lytham St Anne's Branch Ancient Worlds Competition**
This competition is run by the Lytham St Anne's branch of the Classical Association and is open to students aged 11–18. They are invited to pitch a documentary on any aspect of the ancient world in 15 minutes or less. The winners share a prize pot of £650.

**Link:** LSA Classical Association Ancient Worlds Competition 2024 (https://lsaclassics.com/guidelines-2/)

**National Latin Spelling Bee**
This annual Latin spelling event is for KS3 students. Schools first conduct their own knock-out rounds based on vocabulary booklets provided and then select their top five students to represent the school in the grand final. Prizes include certificates, book vouchers and trophies.

**Link:** National Latin Spelling Bee 2024 (https://classicalassociation.org/events/national-latin-spelling-bee-2024/)

Ovid Competition

This competition is run by the Cambridge School Classics Project and is open to UK students in Year 7. Free Classics Tales resources are provided for classwork on Ovid's *Metamorphoses* and then students produce their own creative response to the myths in one of four categories:

1. performance
2. artefact
3. creative writing
4. animation.

Entries are welcome from individual students and groups of up to four. Each school can submit one entry per category. Regional winners receive certificates and badges and the overall winners receive a school prize of £200.

**Link:** Cambridge Schools Classics Project Ovid Competition (https://classictales.co.uk/ovid-competition)

# CHAPTER 4
# HOW CAN I DEVELOP READING, WRITING AND SPEAKING SKILLS IN CLASSICS?

## Reading

Teachers can forget how difficult reading is and sometimes take the process of reading for granted. Reading to learn is also more cognitively demanding than just skimming through a text, as the reader has to read the passage, sometimes several times, to ascertain the meaning, organise the content within a coherent frame of meaning, connect the information to prior knowledge stored in long-term memory and have the motivation to recall and use the information later (Grabe and Yamashita, 2022). Effective reading comprehension therefore comprises several factors: fluency, vocabulary, background knowledge, active reading skills and critical thinking (Teng, 2022). This poses a challenge for both reading in a second language such as Latin and Greek and for reading Classical Civilisation and Ancient History sources, which contain unfamiliar contexts, characters and specialist terminology.

### Preparation is key

The set-up of any reading task needs to be planned with the level of expertise of the students in mind, to enable them to complete the task successfully. Before reading a passage, whether in English, Latin or Greek, we should activate students' prior knowledge through retrieval and discuss the context of the passage, encouraging students to guess what might happen based on this knowledge. We have also already explored how pre-teaching vocabulary, cultural and historical context and characters supports learning by developing students' schemata and this is particularly important when reading unfamiliar texts.

Some Latin and Greek textbooks support this process through pictures or introductions that provide context for the passage and give some indication of what will happen. However, they are not always consistent or offer sufficient information for our students' needs. If you are feeling artistic (and have the time), one way to introduce students to a story is to provide them with a visual representation of the story or storyboard before they translate it. An example of one that Dixon prepared for her Year 10 students when translating a story from *Suburani* is provided through the QR code. It is a good example of how, even when the quality of the drawing is poor, students enjoy working out what the story is about and they then find it much easier to read through the text.

Introductions can also be used to aid comprehension of sources in English by providing context and suggesting what to expect. Reading notes that include definitions of key terminology and contextual information, such as people or events mentioned, can also be provided to support reading, particularly if students are being asked to read material on their own. As already discussed in chapter 3, this is particularly important when using flipped learning to teach set texts.

To further support students' comprehension of a passage, they should have a clear goal for their reading. This could be to answer comprehension questions, provide a direct translation, write summary notes on the passage or find examples from the text to support or oppose an argument. Each outcome requires a different focus while reading, so asking students to read a text and simply 'make notes' can be overwhelming. Moreover, conscientious students will end up making notes on everything, whereas others will make few notes, as they do not know what is important.

## Metacognitive reading strategy

Metacognition is often described as 'thinking about thinking'. It has been shown to be a powerful tool for improving learning and motivation in the classroom (Perry et al., 2019) and is a strong predictor of learning success (Wang et al., 1990). Moreover, it is crucial for strategic reading (Almasi and King Fullerton, 2012; Grabe and Yamashita, 2022) and is the highest ranked strategy on the EEF's Teaching and Learning Toolkit, with teaching reading comprehension strategies ranked second.

**Link:** Education Endowment Foundation, Teaching and Learning Toolkit (https://educationendowmentfoundation.org.uk/education-evidence/teaching-learning-toolkit)

Metacognition supports reading by asking students to question themselves and their understanding of the text throughout the process. It may come naturally to some students but should be taught to all so that it becomes more natural over time. The process below details a metacognitive reading process for before, during and after reading a text. The process and wording of the questions can be varied, depending on the subject and age of students. The questions can be displayed on the board as a prompt while completing a reading task and can be removed gradually once students start to think metacognitively on their own initiative. This process can be used to read texts in English or in Latin and Greek.

### Before reading

Students complete a retrieval task to recall prior knowledge relevant to the passage. They consider the context of the passage and what they think might happen in it so as to provide a framework on which to base their understanding as they read. They also use their prior knowledge of the topic, understanding of the context and the instructions for the task to reflect on whether they have seen similar tasks before and, if so, what strategies they used to complete them.

**Metacognitive questions:**

- What do I already know about this topic?
- Where have I seen this author or context before?
- What do I think might happen based on my prior knowledge and the context?
- What is my aim in reading the passage?
- What strategies could I use to overcome any problems in understanding that I might encounter?

### During reading

It is vital for students to monitor what they are reading, as weaker readers tend not to stop during a task to check that they understand what they are reading (Mokhtari and Reichard, 2002). Students check their understanding of the passage while they read by asking themselves if what they are reading makes sense and if they are on track to complete the task set. If necessary, the teacher reminds students of the strategies available to them for overcoming problems in comprehension either verbally or by displaying a list on the board. These strategies might include using the dictionary to look up unfamiliar vocabulary, re-reading sentences or paragraphs to make sure they have understood what is being said, highlighting or annotating key points, or making a list of things they are unsure about.

**Metacognitive questions:**

- Do I understand what I am reading?
- What strategies can I use to overcome difficulties in understanding what I am reading?

### After reading

Once students finish a reading task, they spend time reflecting on what they understood from it, what worked and what they might need to do differently next time, before discussing this with the class. The teacher checks through students' answers and gives feedback and corrections where necessary.

**Metacognitive questions:**

- What did I understand from this passage?
- What worked well about how I read the passage?
- What could I do differently next to time to help me when reading a similar passage?

## Reading Latin and Greek

How do we 'read' Latin and Greek? Teachers and students can often have an incomplete understanding of the reading process itself and subsequently set unrealistic goals that lead to frustration when reading (Markus and Ross, 2004). A model of reading developed by Gagne (1985) divides the process into four subtasks:

1 decoding
2 literal comprehension
3 inferential comprehension
4 comprehension monitoring.

The lower-level skills involved in decoding and literal comprehension rely on the limited capacity of working memory but can be supported through tasks that strengthen recall from long-term memory and develop automaticity. Hamilton (1991) suggests using the following activities to develop these skills in our students when reading Latin or Greek:

- Practise identifying and matching similar words or word patterns, linked to etymological roots or prefixes, for example. Online quizzes

and resources are useful here for providing a higher frequency of words tested.
- Read the text aloud, as verbal cues may activate memory in different ways from solely reading the written word.
- Explore the meaning of words in the context of a passage, not just in a vocabulary list, to build schemata.
- Relate what is read to the context of the passage but also to the context of the sentence itself to improve predictions about what will happen.

The success of the higher-level skills of inferential comprehension (the process by which information from the passage is integrated, summarised and elaborated to create meaning) and comprehension monitoring (which is closely linked to the metacognitive strategies already discussed) are heavily dependent on a student's understanding of the wider cultural context (Hamilton, 1991). Teaching the background civilisation knowledge is therefore more than just a nice perk for a lesson on a Friday afternoon or at the end of a unit and is vital for providing students with the knowledge required to make links and inferences from what they read and to enable them to understand the meaning of a passage.

## Visualisation

The process of visualising when reading in our own language is so automated that we are often unaware that we are doing it and may not appreciate its importance. However, Quintilian, a first-century AD Roman educator, was fully aware of the benefits of visualisation:

> *For oratory fails of its full effect, and does not assert itself as it should, if its appeal is merely to the hearing, and if the judge merely feels that the facts on which he has to give his decision are being narrated to him, and not displayed in their living truth to the eyes of the mind.*
>
> (Quintilian, *Inst.* 8.3.62, translation from Lacus Curtius)

And he judged Cicero to be the best at it: '*plurimum in hoc genere sicut ceteris eminet Cicero*' (*Inst.* 8.3.64).

Markus and Ross (2004) propose that visualisation of the word-order patterns in the text (integration), the entire passage (summarisation) and the background knowledge of the text (elaboration) can support the development of comprehension. However, this visualisation is much harder to do in a second language.

Visualisation can incorporate both imagining and drawing, two of the generative learning strategies identified by Fiorella and Mayer (2015) which encourage students to select, organise and integrate verbal, textual and visual information to create stronger schemata (Enser and Enser, 2020). Encouraging students to create a mental movie to visualise the events of a passage (Markus and Ross, 2004), as well as either verbally describing or physically jotting down doodles of what they envisage is happening as they read the passage, may help build and strengthen comprehension. Storyboards can also be used, not just as a 'fun' activity, but as a task with real pedagogical value for developing comprehension, improving retention and promoting metacognition (Swalec, 2023).

A proforma that contains a set number of boxes and sentences taken from the story for translation could be given to support students of lower prior attainment and introduce them to this type of task. However, once they are familiar with what is expected in a storyboard task, students can instead be asked to create their own and to include Latin phrases from the story to caption their drawings. The more generative nature of this version of a storyboard task encourages students to engage fully with the Latin themselves and to consolidate their understanding through the process of summarisation.

Storyboard That is a free digital tool that can be used by students to animate and caption stories ([www.storyboardthat.com/](www.storyboardthat.com/)).

## Reading like an ancient

For many, reading Latin and Greek is a decoding process whereby vocabulary and grammatical forms (subject, verb, object) are identified to match the Latin to English grammatical structures and produce a sentence that we hope makes sense. However, this is not how these languages were intended to be read (or more often listened to) and this analytical process can hide contextual clues provided by the sentence itself. McCaffrey found that between 60% and 80% of the time, ambiguous forms in Latin can be resolved by looking back at what has already been read without the need to read ahead: '[Roman authors] are clearly considerate of their audience's mental processes and capacity. They may tease their reader's mental processes and make them work their brains, but they will not mislead them.' (2009, p. 65). The benefits of reading Latin from left to right with a GCSE Latin class are explored by Russell (2018), who introduced the process to her Year 10 class over a series of four lessons.

**Link:** 'Read like a Roman: Teaching students to read in Latin word order' (www.cambridge.org/core/journals/journal-of-classics-teaching/article/read-like-a-roman-teaching-students-to-read-in-latin-word-order/73AB9EA656B8B865FB849E8D5B912D5A)

When reading this way, students should be aware of the basic expectations of Latin syntax, which will help them make predictions of what the complete Latin sentence might look like. Markus and Ross (2004) summarise these expectations as:

- A DIRECT OBJECT raises the expectation of an active verb and of a subject.
- A VERB raises the expectation of a subject and possibly a direct object.
- A SUBJECT raises the expectation of a verb and possibly a direct object.
- A COORDINATING CONJUNCTION raises the expectation of a second syntactic equivalent.
- A SUBORDINATING CONJUNCTION raises an expectation of a finite dependent clause in addition to the independent (main) clause.
- An INFINITIVE raises an expectation of a verb that governs it.
- An ADJECTIVE raises the expectation of a noun to modify in the same case, number and gender.
- A GENITIVE noun raises the expectation of another noun to modify.
- A PREPOSITIONAL PHRASE or an ADVERB raises an expectation of a verb, adjective or another adverb to modify.
- A NOUN in the ABLATIVE or DATIVE raises an expectation of a verb, adjective or rarely an adverb to modify or pattern with.

These expectations can be discussed verbally or written down by annotating the text to lessen the burden on working memory. The skills can also be developed by asking students to predict what will happen in a sentence from its beginning, such as in the following exercise adapted from Markus and Ross.

> **Latin prediction exercise – A-level Latin**
> What can you predict about the sentence from its beginning?
>
> 1  *omnem* ... – <u>somebody/something acts upon (e.g. sees/asks)</u> every <u>thing/person</u>.
>
> 2  *virum qui captus* ... – <u>someone acts upon</u> the man who, having been captured, <u>does something</u>.
>
> 3  *cives in foro* ...
>
> 4  *multos subito* ...
>
> 5  *patri iuvenis* ...

### Embedded reading

In the process of embedded reading three, or sometimes more, scaffolded versions of the same text are read by the class, starting with the text in its simplest form, then an intermediary version, followed by the original (for a step-by-step guide, see Sears and Ballestrini, 2019). The aim is for students to build their confidence as they read through each version. The meaning and context that are gained from the earlier versions help students to read the original text once they reach it. Embedded reading is more often used in the US, but it has also been found to support A-level students of lower prior attainment to understand set texts (Gall, 2020). However, limited lesson time and the strain that creating such resources places on teachers make their use difficult in many classrooms (Hunt, 2022).

**Link:** Toda-lly Comprehensible Latin: Embedded Reading, Part 1 (https://todallycomprehensiblelatin.blogspot.com/)

### Secondary scholarship

Both A-level Classical Civilisation and Ancient History require engagement with secondary scholarship, although this is done in a different way for each. Preparing for this part of the examination can be daunting for both teachers and students, particularly if the teacher is a non-specialist or not confident themselves in engaging with classical scholarship.

## Classical Civilisation

For A-level Classical Civilisation, students must recall quotations from secondary scholarship and incorporate them into their argument in the 30-mark essay question. The mark schemes are vague about what exactly this entails, but Alex Orgee at OCR has published a blog about what is required to satisfy the higher assessment levels. Acceptable secondary scholarship can include podcasts such as *In Our Time*, lectures given by academics (either in person or online), academic books and journals and *Omnibus* articles. Students are expected to reference at least two different scholars and engage with these to further their argument, either by agreeing or disagreeing with the viewpoint of the scholar.

**Link:** 'The scholarship requirement in A Level Classical Civilisation' (www.ocr.org.uk/blog/the-scholarship-requirement-in-alevel-classical-civilisation/)

Students do not have to read the secondary scholarship themselves to be able to complete this task; teachers could just provide them with quotations on the key themes, which they then incorporate into their answers. However, for students who have the time, interest and confidence with reading, this is an ideal opportunity to prepare them for reading academic texts and to expand their subject knowledge. The reading-comprehension strategies already discussed can be used to ease students into reading more academic texts.

The difficulty of this exercise is that the students must (a) understand the arguments put forward by the scholars they read, (b) also be able to accurately recall relevant scholarship in the examination and (c) successfully incorporate into their argument what they quote. The examiners report that weaker answers tend to shoehorn in references to scholarship that are not relevant to the question or do not successfully integrate the quotation into their argument.

Model answers and scaffolding can be used to develop students' understanding of what is required and how to address this aspect of the 30-mark essay question. A range of activities can also be used to strengthen students' recall of secondary scholars and their arguments. For example, to practise engaging with what scholars say, a simple starter task could:

- provide them with a quotation
- ask them to give evidence from the sources studied to say whether they agree with the argument or not.

## Starter task to revise secondary scholarship – A-level Classical Civilisation

'The enthralling contest between god and man is arguably the play's most immediate attraction, but of equal importance are the philosophical and theological questions embedded in it.' Mills, S. (2006) *Euripides: Bacchae*

How far do you agree with Mills's statement? Write a list of points from the text that you could use to either agree or disagree with her point.

A fill-in-the-gaps worksheet could also be used as a scaffolded recall task.

## Fill in the gaps recall – A-level Classical Civilisation

Complete the quotations with key words from the grey boxes below. Pick your three favourite quotations and explain why you agree with what the scholar has said, based on your reading of Sappho's poems.

| 1 | Important ____ purpose and public function. (Judith Hallett) |
| --- | --- |
| 2 | Celebrated as the mortal ____ . (Antipater of Sidon) |
| 3 | So that I may ____ it then die. (Solon of Athens) |
| 4 | Sappho does not picture love relations as ____ by one partner over the other. (Ellen Greene) |
| 5 | Sappho can represent an ____ for women to the cultural norms. (Eva Stehle) |
| 6 | I am fascinated by the way she takes on ____ – and subverts him. (Charlotte Higgins) |
| 7 | Sappho's ____ stance, in the ancient setting, was unremarkable. (Edith Hall) |
| 8 | She is the poetess who addressed more than anyone the ____ from girlhood to womanhood. (Andromache Karanika) |
| 9 | Sappho deeply communicates the female anxiety towards ____ , ____ that did not operate in any romantic terms that we see today. (Andromache Karanika) |
| 10 | The universality of ____ is why she's so enduring. (Andromache Karanika) |

95

| transition | emotion | learn | Muse | domination |
| alternative | marriage | Homer | homoerotic | social |

**Recall of scholarship**

A graphic organiser template could be used to practise the recall of secondary scholarship quotations:

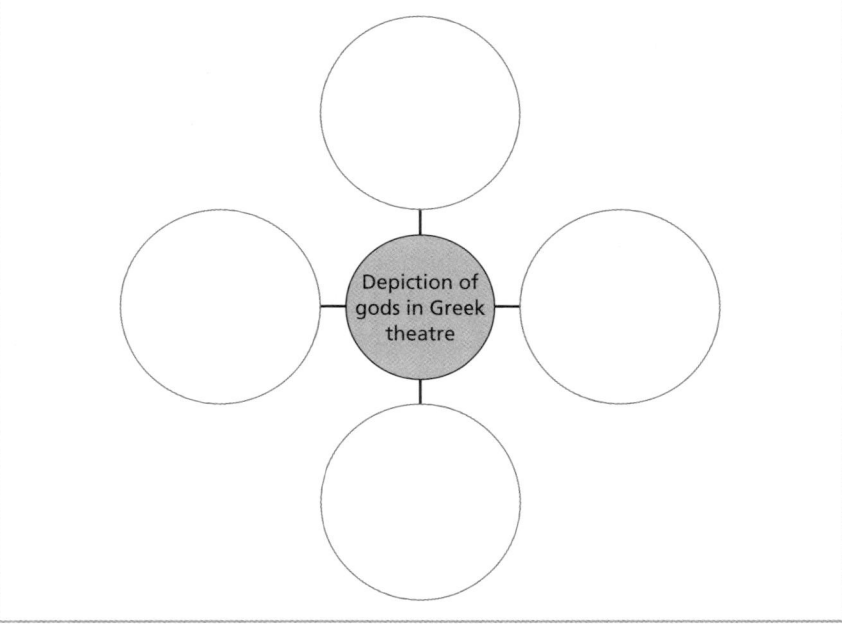

**Graphic organiser to revise secondary scholarship – A-level Classical Civilisation**

Fill each circle with a quotation from a secondary scholar on the depiction of the gods in Greek theatre. Annotate each circle with detail from the text that you think either proves or disproves the scholars' points.

Depiction of gods in Greek theatre

In the following case study, Danny Pucknell explains an activity he uses with his students.

# Case study of the secondary scholarship jeopardy grid in A-level Classical Civilisation
## Danny Pucknell, Cardiff and Vale College

This activity is conceived as a way of consolidating multiple examples of scholarship at once. It was a task which my colleagues and I originally began using to check subject knowledge while teaching History and Government and Politics but later adapted to check recall of scholarship for themes, ideas or people in A-level Classical Civilisation. I often use it at the end of a term or half term, to solidify the scholarship which has been learned over that period.

The task works well as a team game and I find my students are extremely competitive, especially when it comes to beating their friends or classmates. Each square in the grid contains the name of a scholar. Students must either give me a quote from that scholar on one of the issues in the exam specification or be able to define their position on an issue or theme.

Split the class in half and as each team gets an answer right, you ring the section in the colour picked by that team. For example:

| Goldsworthy | Balcer | Brunt |
|---|---|---|
| Zanker | Smith | Crawford |
| Beard | Pollini | Eck |
| Edwards | Kagan | Meier |

The team with the most rings on the grid at the end wins. Alternatively, this can be used as a pair or individual revision resource, where a student uses a copy of the grid to check whether they have some usable scholarship for all the individuals listed.

The grids can also be used in reverse to check the level of scholarship students possess related to particular individuals or theories within a module. For example, the grid below would relate to those studying 'Belief and Ideas in the Roman Republic'.

CLASSICS IN ACTION

| Julius Caesar | Marius | Cato |
| --- | --- | --- |
| 'The Elastic Band Theory' | Pompey | Marcus Crassus |
| Sulla | Mark Anthony | Octavian |
| Cicero | 'The Cult of the General' | Lucullus |

If a teacher wanted to consider the growth of the power of individual politicians as a cause of the decline and collapse of the Republic, they could ask students to select one of the individuals or theories in this grid and give an example of a piece of scholarship relating to it. For example, in order to take Pompey off the grid, students might cite the work of Seager, who describes the growth of Pompey's power and wealth as a result of his campaigns against Mithridates.

If this resource is used as a consolidation exercise and builds upon efforts by teachers to embed scholarship across the academic year, it gives students a realistic understanding of how much scholarship they have retained and where they may need to focus their future revision of secondary scholarship.

### Ancient History

In A-level Ancient History, students are provided with a passage from a secondary scholar on the examination paper and are asked how convincing they find the scholar's view, based on their own understanding of the sources. The examiners are looking for answers that engage with the scholar's interpretation, rather than solely narrate the content of what is said. Students of Ancient History therefore need to develop competent reading comprehension skills, so they can accurately read and interpret the argument of an unknown quotation from a secondary scholar in the examination, as well as the ability to write a concise critique of these arguments.

Many of the strategies already discussed can be used to develop these skills, such as the metacognitive reading strategy, model answers, scaffolding, blurt it out, etc. Starter tasks that ask students to read and annotate an extended passage from a secondary scholar in a set time will be of particular benefit for being able to interpret unfamiliar texts quickly in the examination. Developing students' academic vocabulary will also be of great importance.

## Academic vocabulary

Students may not have the range of vocabulary required to read set texts and secondary scholarship, especially if they contain subject-specific terminology that students are unlikely to have met. Easy ways to develop vocabulary include giving students lists of key terminology, identifying new words in context, building a class glossary of new words and regular terminology tests.

Rewordify is a free website that identifies difficult vocabulary in a text and suggests simplified vocabulary and definitions. It can help teachers identify vocabulary that we, as experts may not realise will be tricky for students to understand.

**Link:** Rewordify, 'Understand what you read' (https://rewordify.com/index.php)

For example, it suggests the following rewording for Appian, *The Civil Wars* 3.92, which is a set text for A-level Ancient History:

| Original | Rewordify version |
| --- | --- |
| While Octavian was still giving audience to the messengers, it was announced to him that the decrees had been rescinded. The messengers withdrew, and returned in embarrassment. With his army still more exasperated, Octavian hastened to the city, fearing something evil might befall his mother and sister. He sent horsemen in advance to tell the agitated population to not be afraid, and in the general state of amazement seized the area just beyond the Quirinal Hill. Now another wonderful and sudden change took place. Patricians flocked out and saluted him; the common people ran also and took the good order of the soldiers for a sign of peace. | While Octavian was still giving audience to the messengers, it was announced to him that the legal statements had been taken back. The messengers withdrew, and returned in embarrassment. With his army still more extremely irritated, Octavian hurried to the city, fearing something evil might happen to his mother and sister. He sent horsemen in advance to tell the upset/angry population to not be afraid, and in the general state of extreme surprise seized the area just beyond the Quirinal Hill. Now another wonderful and sudden change happened. Rich people moved (in large numbers) out and saluted him; the common people ran also and took the good order of the soldiers for a sign of peace. |

This tool can be used to create pre-teaching tasks that focus on defining and developing vocabulary knowledge before a text is read.

CLASSICS IN ACTION

## Vocabulary match-up exercise – A-level Classical Civilisation

Match up the vocabulary in the first column with the definitions in the second.

| Vocabulary | Definition |
|---|---|
| 1  decrees | A  hurried |
| 2  rescind | B  upset/angry |
| 3  exasperated | C  legal statements |
| 4  hasten | D  extremely angry/upset |
| 5  befall | E  rich people |
| 6  agitated | F  moving in large numbers |
| 7  amazement | G  take back |
| 8  patricians | H  happen |
| 9  flocked | I  extreme surprise |

Students can also be asked to find the words in the passage and give their own definitions from the context.

## Vocabulary definition task – A-level Ancient History

Highlight the given vocabulary in the passage and write a definition of what you think the word means based on the context of the passage.

While Octavian was still giving audience to the messengers, it was announced to him that the decrees had been rescinded. The messengers withdrew, and returned in embarrassment. With his army still more exasperated, Octavian hastened to the city, fearing something evil might befall his mother and sister. He sent horsemen in advance to tell the agitated population to not be afraid, and in the general state of amazement seized the area just beyond the Quirinal Hill. Now another wonderful and sudden change took place. Patricians flocked out and saluted him; the common people ran also and took the good order of the soldiers for a sign of peace.

| Vocabulary | Definition |
|---|---|
| 1 decrees | |
| 2 rescind | |
| 3 exasperated | |
| 4 hasten | |
| 5 befall | |
| 6 agitated | |
| 7 amazement | |
| 8 patricians | |
| 9 flocked | |

# Writing

## Latin and Greek

### Translation

The nature of translation was much discussed following the publication of Emily Wilson's translation of the *Odyssey* in (2017). In an interview for the Runciman award in 2018, she argued that 'pedagogy tends to rely heavily on "translation" as a tool that stands in for comprehension'. A line of Latin and Greek can be translated word by word into an English sentence without the translator understanding what is being said. Indeed, it can often feel like this when marking student translations, particularly when they first meet the standard of A-level unseens. There is a distinction therefore between translating a passage and truly reading it, which requires comprehension.

The production of a written translation is an important form of assessment at GCSE and A-level and, while mark schemes allow examiners to accept any approach that 'satisfactorily conveys the meaning of the Latin', the examiners' crucial consideration is 'the extent to which every Latin word is satisfactorily rendered in some way in the English' (OCR mark scheme for A-level Latin Paper 1, Unseen translation, 2022). Students can often fixate on producing the 'correct' translation and become bogged down in rendering Latin word-for-word into English without truly understanding what is being said or without even producing a translation that makes sense in English. How, then, can teachers encourage students to produce translations that are accurate enough to satisfy the marking guidelines set out by examiners but also show understanding and render an accurate interpretation of the meaning of the passage?

**Translation best practice**
Before attempting a translation, students should look at the additional information provided in the introduction in English and the list of names and glossed vocabulary. They should then read through the passage, ideally out loud to gain an overview of what the passage is about before putting pen to paper. On the second read-through they should annotate the text to show main verbs, subordinate clauses, prepositional phrases, constructions, etc., and to highlight vocabulary they do not know or phrases they are unsure about. By reading through the passage several times, the context of what comes later will hopefully help them make better guesses for any vocabulary they are uncertain about. Finally, they should write out their translation, regularly going back to check for understanding and ensure that their answer makes sense (Praet and Verhelst, 2020). See also Hunt (2022) for further discussion of translation best practice.

**Translation theory**
Translation theory is often taught at university level either as a practical translation course for language students, for example at Ghent University (Praet and Verhelst, 2020), or to understand the role of translation in classical reception, such as at Durham University.

**Link:** Programme and Module Handbook: Undergraduate Programme and Module Handbook 2022–2023 (archived) (https://apps.dur.ac.uk/faculty.handbook/2022/UG/module/CLAS1701)

At school level, students can be asked to compare different translations to see how differences in the translator's gender, purpose or the time at which they were writing may have affected their work. Emily Wilson's translations of the *Odyssey* and *Iliad* are key resources for this task. The comparisons can either be done fully in translation with a Classical Civilisation class or can include the original Latin or Greek for language students. Further discussion and comparison can also be made about how these versions have been adapted and reproduced visually and in film. Example resources are shared through the QR code. An additional visual task could ask students to compare ancient depictions of Penelope, such as the terracotta plaque showing Odysseus returning to

Penelope (Melian, 460–450BC), with later depictions of the myth, such as Pinturicchio's *Penelope with the Suitors* (c. 1509) and John Roddam Spencer Stanhope's *Penelope* (1864).

## Prose composition

As discussed in chapter 1, prose composition is an optional skill that can be examined at GCSE and A-level For those schools that do teach prose composition, some introduce it from the beginning of a language course, particularly when using grammar–translation textbooks such as the Oxford Latin Course or Taylor's *Latin* or *Greek to GCSE* textbooks that provide English-to-Latin practice in each chapter. Others, however, begin to teach it only when students reach GCSE or A-level, in order to prepare them for the optional prose composition elements in the examinations.

Scaffolded resources and guided practice are invaluable for helping students gain confidence in prose composition and lessons can be learned from colleagues in MFL departments on how to prepare effective resources. Particularly at GCSE, vocabulary should either be provided or be kept simple to reduce cognitive load. A common method is to model sentences on ones that students have already translated, either alternating sentences from Latin–English to closely related English–Latin or as a separate exercise. This allows students to use the vocabulary and grammar provided in the Latin–English sentences as a model. However, unless the two sentences are very closely related, this task will still be difficult for students who do not already have a firm understanding of Latin accidence and are not able to relate what they see in the Latin sentences to the English that is to be translated.

### Sentence builders

Sentence builders reduce the cognitive load for students by providing them with the building blocks needed to create their sentences. An easy extension task is then to ask students to create sentences with vocabulary not listed. Below are some simple sentence-builder exercises followed by a case study by Lottie Mortimer, detailing more a complex sentence-builder task.

## Sentence builder – KS3 Latin

Choose one Latin word from each column to match the English sentence above.

*The cruel general punished the soldiers because they lost his money.*

| imperator | crudeles | militem | punivit | ubi | pecuniam | eius | amittunt |
| imperatorem | crudelis | milites | puniebat | quod | pecuniae | eis | amiserunt |

## Sentence builder – KS3 Latin

1. Use the table below to write four sentences in Latin that include a dative case noun. Keep a record of what you think the sentences should mean in English and ask your partner to translate them to check your compositions. Some words are singular and some are plural, so check the endings carefully.

| Nominative | Dative | Accusative | Verb |
| --- | --- | --- | --- |
| *liberi* | *liberis* | *liberos* | *dedit, dederunt* |
| *filia* | *filiae* | *filiam* | *ostendit, ostenderunt* |
| *amicus* | *amico* | *amicum* | *offerebat, offerebant* |
| *templum* | *templo* | *templum* | *emebat, emebant* |
| *fabulae* | *fabulis* | *fabulas* | *narravit, narraverunt* |

2. Write three more sentences in Latin that include a dative case noun, but this time use different first and second declension nouns from those listed above (some suggestions are given below, but use any that you know). Use the table to help you with the case endings.

First and second declension nouns:

*puella, femina, cena, turba, dea*

*dominus, servus, nuntius, praemium, signum*

# Case study of using sentence builders to help students write their own stories

Lottie Mortimer, University of Sussex

Teaching compounds of the verb *eo* provided an excellent opportunity to revise prepositions and get students writing in Latin. Instead of giving students endless sentences to practise, I wanted my students to explore the words with pictures and stories.

I created an image of an island and populated it with various features using simple pictures that I found online. I then wrote a short story about two characters and their adventure around the island. As students read the story, they annotated the picture with the journeys of the two characters. I modelled this task with the first two sentences, so that students understood how to do the task.

I then asked students to draw their own island. I provided them with a selection of vocabulary of geographic features, of which they needed to include at least six. These are the words that I would include in my sentence builder later on. As a challenge, some students used Latin dictionaries to add their own unique vocabulary. Afterwards, I asked students to create their own character. I provided scaffolds in Latin to help write an introduction about them such as '*hic/haec/hoc est [name]*'. Alongside this I provided my own example as a model.

It was then time for students to write their own stories in Latin about their islands. Writing in Latin can be quite overwhelming, as there are so many things that students need to think about. Not only do they have to remember the correct vocabulary, but they then must inflect it correctly. To scaffold this task, I created a sentence builder, which I had been inspired to try after their implementation by our MFL department. The vocabulary was set out in columns: (adverb), nominative noun, preposition, accusative/ablative noun and verb. The order of the columns reflected the order of the words in Latin sentences. The words were already inflected and I provided a translation underneath each one (which could be removed to provide additional challenge). Students picked a word from each column to construct their sentences to write their story. Students were not limited to the vocabulary on the sentence builder and those who included additional features on their island needed to inflect their own nouns.

Afterwards, students swapped stories with their partner and verbally talked through each other's stories using the image. An alternative to this would have been to ask students to translate each other's stories.

Sometimes students can find writing Latin an overwhelming process. The cognitive load is very high, as there are so many different things that students need to think about to craft accurate Latin sentences. This task was engaging and students found it very enjoyable, many pushing themselves to add additional vocabulary or building more complex sentences. The sentence builder enabled students to encounter and put together a lot of Latin in a short space of time, and the accompanying pictures made it even more memorable. We also know that stories are particularly powerful when it comes to memory.

The resource for this exercise is shared through the following QR code.

### Literary analysis

At both GCSE and A-level, students need to develop literary analysis skills to evaluate how authors use their style of writing to enrich a text and amplify their meaning. At GCSE, most schools do not start teaching the Latin literature texts until students have mastered the grammar requirements of the course, which is often the end of Year 10 or even the start of Year 11. As a result, students may already be halfway through their GCSE course before they meet original Latin literature and learn how to analyse texts. However, these skills can and should be introduced and developed during KS3, so they are not such a shock once students start engaging with the set texts. They are also a way to promote engagement and interest in learning Latin as a means to understanding literature.

The following case studies by Lottie Mortimer and Henry Cullen consider approaches to developing literary analysis first in KS3 and then at GCSE and A-level.

# Case study of introducing Latin literature at KS3 using dual translation

**Lottie Mortimer, University of Sussex**

Literature is sometimes seen as one of the most difficult but enjoyable parts of studying Latin. I therefore believe it's important to start developing students' Latin literature skills before they encounter literature at GCSE. This means that students can start to build these skills gradually and they can start to appreciate texts as texts rather than as translation or comprehension exercises. All Latin courses, whether reading or grammar–translation, contain stories that can be used to introduce students to literature analysis early on in their Latin learning journey.

Firstly, it's important to pick a good story and decide a key question to be the focus which will 'hook' students in. A story which I find works well is *fabula mirabilis* from Stage 7 of *Cambridge Latin Course* Book 1, focusing on how the author builds suspense. This can tie in with work students do on gothic horror in their English lessons, establishing meaningful cross-curricular links.

I set an initial exercise when we first read through the story, so that students start to familiarise themselves with the plot and the language before moving on to analysis. This could include teacher questioning, a cloze exercise or scaffolded translation. This is also a great opportunity to reflect on their initial reactions to the text. We then start our analysis. Depending on the question, I might explore some of the key features that they might be expecting to find in that genre beforehand, allowing me to check their prior knowledge. I always provide students with an A4 or A3 sheet with the Latin text printed in the middle of the left-hand side and an English translation printed similarly on the right. This dual translation is important, as it means that everyone in the class has the same version of the story to refer to and the same starting point.

After we model one or two examples as a class using the visualiser, students then work in pairs to highlight interesting features of the text with a focus on the question. I don't mind if students start with the English text and then find the corresponding Latin to match, as the point of this exercise is to get students to think about the story as a piece of literature, not just something to translate. Some students might be able to identify features from the Latin straightaway. Whichever approach students take, I want the same example highlighted in both the Latin and the English and one of them to have an annotation to explain what they have highlighted.

We then come together as a class and discuss the examples that we found. We might leave the story there or move on to writing a PEA (point, evidence, analysis) paragraph to answer the key question. The highlighting exercise and class discussion have provided a scaffold, so that students have the information needed to write a paragraph about the text. I would usually scaffold this task further, with sentence starters for each step and modelling an example before students write their own paragraphs using their favourite examples from the text. I make it clear that the examples that students use in their quote must be in Latin. After this, students can swap paragraphs to give peer feedback to each other.

Although students can be initially sceptical of this type of task, these lessons have resulted in comments such as 'that was the best Latin lesson, can we do that again?' multiple times. It's great to watch students identify features of the text that I haven't thought of myself.

Suggested stories with which you could introduce literary analysis in KS3 are shared through the QR code.

## Case study of scaffolding 'style' analysis at GCSE and A-level
### Henry Cullen, St Albans High School for Girls

What is 'style', for the purposes of school-level analysis of Latin and Greek texts? Certainly, much more than the tedious trainspotting of a list of literary devices. Of course, ancient authors often did purposefully deploy flourishes such as anaphora, alliteration and so on. But approaching 'style' primarily through this lens can miss much of what is most interesting about a passage. It also can lead students to fixate, unhelpfully, on just the technical aspect of 'style': less confident literary critics cling on to these bits of jargon as a comfort blanket and are often delighted to point a device out, only to be at a loss as to how to explain its actual effect upon the reader. More confident literary critics, meanwhile, can find themselves trotting out formulaic 'style comments' entirely geared around the technical terms; these may get full marks in an exam question but also serve to limit their engagement with a text.

So, what is 'style' in my book? To start students off, I have found it helpful to ask three simple (perhaps simplistic) questions to get them thinking in different ways about a passage:

1. What is – crudely – the author's 'aim' in these lines?
2. What is the simplest way the author could have expressed this?
3. How and where has the author deliberately deviated from, or elaborated upon, this?

In the answer to question 3 lies 'style' – any artful, *chosen* deployment of information and language in such a way as to affect a reader's or listener's reaction as they work through a line or sentence. Articulating answers to these three questions can often get a student a long way towards formulating their oral or written analysis of what's interesting about a passage: not just an author's rhetorical tricks, but, zooming out a little, their tactics more broadly.

What sort of things can students be looking out for which are most worthy of 'style' comment?

Long before any thought of a list of devices, the principal 'stylistic' technique at an ancient author's disposal was word order. This fact can seem rather pedestrian for the GCSE student who is itching to expound on (e.g.) anaphora, but word order is arguably the most important thing of all to watch out for. By far the best way to demonstrate to students the artful – but often easily missed – effects of word order is to read out the English translation, as much as possible, in exactly the same word order as the Latin or Greek. What is an author seeking to achieve with unusual word order? Early verbs, early accusatives, tacked on extra details, masterly delay of key facts by the use of subordinate clauses, delayed nominatives – all become easier to spot when reading aloud this way.

To encourage students to embrace the many different layers of 'style', have them analyse the same passage with different 'lenses':

1. the essential content (the 'skeleton') of a passage versus additional details that are not strictly necessary but are added for effect
2. any interesting – i.e. non-normal – word order
3. any interesting diction – either individual words of resonance or patterns
4. anything of particular historical or cultural resonance
5. finally – unleash that list of literary devices.

A sample illustration of such an approach for a section of the recent *Pro Cluentio* A-level set text can be accessed through the QR code. You can analyse the same passage repeatedly, each time applying a different filter and annotating it in a different way. As you can see, there is plenty to comment on just by applying lenses 1–4, before we even begin to consider the rhetorical devices. It is of course impractical to cover every section of a text in this exhaustive way. But to do so occasionally – especially at the outset of studying a text – tends to open students' eyes as to what 'style' can comprise and helps them generate a range of insights about a text. It is certainly preferable to the tedious trainspotting and a much richer discussion often ensues.

## Classical Civilisation and Ancient History

### Source analysis

Students at both GCSE and A-level have to engage with a range of source material to draw out the information they present to us and to evaluate their usefulness and limitations. This requires the ability to read and understand the language and nuance of a source, as well as having an understanding of not just the nature of the source itself, remembering dates, locations and authors with unfamiliar names, but also of what makes a source accurate and reliable.

The requirements and marking criteria for source analysis vary for each subject and level, but generally students should know and be able to explain:

- the provenance of a source
- the contemporary context
- its intended purpose and audience
- if any information is exaggerated or omitted
- if the source is damaged and how this affects its usefulness or reliability
- how the source compares or contrasts with other sources studied.

These concepts can at first be difficult for students new to Classics to grasp while they build their schemata of chronology, names and places.

Moreover, they will need to be shown how to write answers that move beyond simply stating whether a source is reliable or useful and instead develop a perceptive and concise analysis of the material.

Scaffolding and model answers will help students develop their written analysis of source material. Retrieval tasks and spaced practice will also strengthen their recall of knowledge about specific sources. Some suggested tasks to develop source analysis are given below, with many explored in more detail in the Mode A/Mode B section.

- Timed annotation of a source to identify points they could make across all the source material provided and any themes on which to frame an answer. This replicates the time the students would have in an exam to read through a given source(s) and make a quick plan of action before starting to write.
- Timelines of sources to show their relationship to the events described and each other.
- Quizzes on factual detail of the sources (author, date, genre, location found, purpose, etc.).
- Blurt it out – write down as much as you can about X source or author.
- Model answers, sentence starters and fill-in-the-blank examples to show students how to integrate source analysis into an essay.

Source analysis grids can be used to guide students towards identifying the content of a source and explaining its usefulness and reliability. They can be done with only a couple of quotations at a time as a starter exercise or be provided as a longer exercise for revision of specific themes.

# Source analysis grid – A-level Ancient History

What do these sources tell us about Augustus' relationship with the senate? Complete the grid to show your understanding. The first is done as an example.

| Quotation | Analysis of content | Evaluation of reliability/usefulness |
|---|---|---|
| I transferred the state from my power into the control of the Roman senate and people. For this service, I was named Augustus by senatorial decree… and a golden shield was set up in the Julian senate-house. (*Res Gestae*) | *Augustus gave power back to the senate and was awarded honours by the senate for doing so = shows a positive relationship.* | *RG is an autobiography and therefore shows how important Augustus thought it was to portray that he had a positive relationship with the senate. However, he exaggerates when he says he transfers power back to the senate and people.* |
| When Augustus presided on this second occasion, he is said to have worn a sword and a steel corselet beneath his tunic. (Suetonius) | | |
| Arrogating to himself the functions of the senate. (Tacitus) | | |
| On one side was Augustus Caesar, leading the Italians to battle together with the Senate and People, the Penates and the great gods. (Virgil) | | |

## Essay writing

Essay-writing skills are required for both Classical Civilisation and Ancient History A-level and to a lesser extent for both subjects at GCSE. Students need to practise writing coherent arguments that bring together and analyse a range of evidence from the sources studied, are based within the historical, social and cultural context, and lead to a convincing conclusion. As discussed earlier in this chapter, A-level Classical Civilisation also requires that students recall and engage with secondary scholarship in their 30-mark essay, all of which must be done within the time limit of the examination.

Crucial for developing these skills in preparation for the examinations are the instructional methods already discussed, such as live modelling, model answers, scaffolds, developing group answers, etc. Class activities to analyse and improve upon the exemplar answers provided by the exam board or examples written by previous cohorts or the teachers themselves can help students to identify and start a dialogue about what works and what doesn't when writing essays.

### Essay-plan scaffolds

An example essay-plan scaffold is provided through the QR code. The first step is to ask students to identify the key words in the question and check that they understand what it is asking them to write about. The scaffold then walks students through the process of recalling and organising factual detail to develop their essay plan and then to identify relevant quotations from secondary scholars and integrate them into their point. Students can then write the essay once they are confident that they have sufficient knowledge and understanding in relation to the question.

### Essay reflection

Strong formative feedback that identifies specific areas for improvement and explains how to achieve this is also vital for students to develop these skills. Students should be encouraged to rewrite weaker sections of essays to implement feedback straightaway, rather than waiting for the next essay to be set. Self-reflection that promotes metacognition is also important for developing essay-writing skills. For example, the essay-reflection sheet below uses the requirements of the mark scheme as a guide for evaluating what worked well and what they need to improve on. The same what-went-well and areas-to-improve grid can be used when assessing exemplar answers provided by the exam board or those written by previous cohorts.

## Essay-reflection sheet – A-level Classical Civilisation

**Essay title:**

**Mark:**

| | What went well | Areas to improve |
|---|---|---|
| *All questions* | • Knowledge of material<br>• Understanding of material<br>• Analysis of material<br>• Engagement with question<br>• Range and relevance of points<br>• Support points with evidence<br>• Development of points | • Knowledge of material<br>• Understanding of material<br>• Analysis of material<br>• Engagement with question<br>• Range and relevance of points<br>• Support points with evidence<br>• Development of points |
| *20- and 30-mark questions* | • Range of sources referred to<br>• Reference to cultural context<br>• Evaluation of classical sources<br>• Development of argument<br>• Conclusion<br>• Structure of response | • Range of sources referred to<br>• Reference to cultural context<br>• Evaluation of classical sources<br>• Development of argument<br>• Conclusion<br>• Structure of response |
| *30-mark questions only* | • Use of secondary scholarship | • Use of secondary scholarship |

| |
|---|
| What did you do when planning and writing this question that worked well? |
| What didn't work so well and what could you do to improve this next time? |
| What further questions do you have about this topic? |

## Creative writing

Classics has always inspired creativity both inside and outside the classroom, through storytelling, drama and art, but especially literature and creative writing. The *Percy Jackson* series by Rick Riordan remains one of the key vehicles through which young people engage with Greek mythology. Caroline Lawrence has inspired school children about the Roman world and the process of storytelling through her *Roman Mysteries* series and writing workshops. Furthermore, the success of novels that have retold classical myths, most often from the female viewpoint, by authors such as Natalie Haynes, Madeline Miller and Pat Barker, has stimulated wider interest in Classics and shown students the possibility of making these myths their own.

Each year, creative-writing competitions, for example those run by the Faculty of Classics at the University of Oxford and by the Classical Association in collaboration with Bloomsbury, help engage young people with Classics and foster a greater passion and sense of awe for the ancient world.

Creative writing can also be used in the classroom to engage students with classical civilisation and culture or to explore the perspectives of characters within set texts (Lucas, 2021). To move students beyond just writing a nice story, engagement can be made with the reception of classical texts and exploration of how mythology and history have been utilised and adapted by modern authors and artists (see Sykes, 2021 for suggested resources).

**Links:** Caroline Lawrence's *Roman Mysteries* and writing workshops (https://carolinelawrence.com/schools/)

The Classical Association Competition (https://classicalassociation.org/competition/)

University of Oxford, Faculty of Classics Creative Writing Competition 2024 (https://clasoutreach.web.ox.ac.uk/creativewriting-2024)

Sykes, R. (2021) 'Can studying a topic through a reception studies approach improve the quality of Year 7 students' creative responses to the ancient world?', *Journal of Classics Teaching*, 22(43), pp. 4–21. (https://doi.org/10.1017/S2058631021000027)

## Speaking

Spoken Latin is not a new concept. W. H. D. Rouse introduced his 'Direct Method' in the 1920s, which saw Latin taught solely in Latin. It is a popular method of teaching in American schools and the benefits of speaking Latin include making lessons more engaging and immersive. However, as speaking and listening skills are not tested in the GCSE and A-level qualifications, spoken Latin is not widely used in UK classrooms and many teachers themselves are not confident with speaking the language.

Where spoken Latin is used, it is often for games and fun activities at KS3. Ana Martin is a staunch advocate of speaking Latin and has promoted its use in numerous summer schools and CPD events. Here she explains how it could be used to enrich GCSE Latin teaching.

**Link:** 'Latin: the Direct Method' (www.arlt.co.uk/history/w-h-d-rouse/the-direct-method/)

# Case study of spoken Latin at GCSE
## Ana Martin, Latin Tutor Online

GCSE Latin examinations may not seem the most obvious space to bring spoken Latin to life: there is no listening component, barely any output in the target language is required from the student and, sadly, not one single opportunity for free expression in Latin is given. However, in my opinion, spoken Latin can and should be included in GCSE preparation. It is a very effective tool to prepare for examination, even in the context of the current OCR GCSE format.

Speaking in Latin is an easy way to consolidate vocabulary, which is the backbone of language comprehension. If, in addition to reading the texts, we also talk about the texts, words are heard in new contexts, manipulated without fear of making mistakes and, most importantly, repeated regularly to aid acquisition. Crucially, texts also gain a purpose beyond a test in translation skills: they become the conversation and are used for communication, which is what we learn languages for in the first place.

Spoken Latin is also the surest path to appreciating the original literature. Unfortunately, it is not uncommon for students to memorise set texts in English and still achieve a good grade. However, this is not particularly educational – what is the skill being acquired? It is, in fact, limiting for there seems to be only one translation of the text, one interpretation of the use of language. Speaking about the text, on the other hand, helps the student identify what makes the choices of the author unique, explore other forms the text may have taken – tiered activities are essential here – and get a real sense of its performative properties.

In both my blog and my YouTube channel you will find examples of the types of activities that foster an active use of the language, making sure all four skills (listening, reading, writing and speaking) are exercised. The resource available through the QR code details how spoken Latin could be used to explore depictions of Aeneas' descent into the underworld in *Aeneid* book 6.

**Links:** blog: www.latintutoronline.com/blog

YouTube channel: www.youtube.com/@latintutoronline

# CHAPTER 5
# WHERE CAN I GO FOR FURTHER HELP AND RESOURCES?

There is a wealth of resources available for teachers who want to develop their teaching of classical subjects. Any list we provide can never be exhaustive, but we hope what we have collected together below provides a helpful basis from which to begin.

## Literature

### Books

Bulwer, J. (ed.) (2006) *Classics Teaching in Europe*. Duckworth.

Gruber-Miller (ed.) (2006) *When Dead Tongues Speak: Teaching Beginning Greek and Latin*. Oxford University Press.

Holmes-Henderson, A. (2023) *Expanding Classics: Practitioner Perspectives from Museums and Schools*. Routledge.

Holmes-Henderson, A., Hunt, S. and M. Musié, (eds.) (2018) *Forward with Classics. Classical Languages in Schools and Communities*. Bloomsbury.

Hunt, S. (2023) *Starting to Teach Latin*. 2nd edn. Bloomsbury.

Hunt, S. (2022) *Teaching Latin: Contexts, Theories, Practices*. Bloomsbury.

Lister, R. (2007) *Changing Classics in Schools*. Cambridge University Press.

Lloyd, M. and Hunt, S. (2020) *Communicative Approaches for Ancient Languages*. Bloomsbury Academic.

Morwood, J. (2003) *The Teaching of Classics*. Cambridge University Press.

Natoli, B. and Hunt, S. (eds.) (2019) *Teaching Classics with Technology*. Bloomsbury.

### Articles

Articles on Classics pedagogy can be found online in:

*Journal of Classics Teaching* (www.cambridge.org/core/journals/journal-of-classics-teaching)

*Teaching Classical Languages* (https://tcl.camws.org/)

*Quinquennium* is a blog on Classics pedagogy and professional development (www.quinquennium.com/about-blog/)

## Resources

The main resource-sharing website for Classics teachers is (currently) the Classics Library, run by ex-Classics teacher Stephen Jenkin. Teachers and trainee teachers should register for access via the log-in page and explore the resources that have been uploaded by practising teachers in each of the subject areas (www.theclassicslibrary.com/)

The Cambridge School Classics Project provides a wide range of textbook-linked resources as well as GCSE teaching and learning materials (www.cambridgescp.com).

Hands Up Education offers support for Latin and Greek learning (https://hands-up-education.org/).

The Open University provides free courses on the classical world on its HeadStart Classical Studies page (www.open.edu/openlearn/history-the-arts/headstart-classical-studies).

Balliol College, Oxford has prepared a reading list for prospective Classics undergraduate students covering literature, history and philosophy (www.balliol.ox.ac.uk/admissions/undergraduate-admissions/classics-reading-lists)

## Videos

Videos, linked to the OCR examination specifications, have been produced by a number of universities. You can view these here:

'The Women of Virgil's *Aeneid*: Part of the epic mission or not?' (www.youtube.com/watch?v=DsbKzzt9cF8)

'Advocating Classics Education' (http://aceclassics.org.uk/resources/syllabus-overviews/)

'Gandhi and the reception history of Plato's *Apology*' (www.youtube.com/watch?v=AdOEhjnL-GU)

Classics and Ancient History @ Warwick (www.youtube.com/@classicsandancienthistoryw3264)

MASSOLIT is a company that provides subscription-based access to high-quality videos that support syllabus content in humanities subjects (https://massolit.io/)

## Organisations

The main subject association for Classics teachers is the Classical Association. It maintains a list of resources for teachers and home-schoolers. It publishes a range of academic journals including the *Journal of Classics Teaching* and *Omnibus* magazine, which is aimed at teachers and sixth-form students. The Classical Association hosts annual CPD days for Classical Civilisation, Ancient History and Latin/Greek and a major annual conference (in a different UK city each year) for which teachers qualify for a reduced registration fee. For more details and to join see: www.classicalassociation.org/

Three additional classical subject associations are worth exploring:

The Society for the Promotion of Roman Studies (www.romansociety.org/)

The Society for the Promotion of Hellenic Studies (www.hellenicsociety.org.uk/)

The key advantage of these two learned societies is membership of the Hellenic and Roman Library at Senate House in London. This library holds a stunning collection of texts and offers a postal loan service for members outside London.

The Association for Latin Teaching (ARLT) (www.arlt.co.uk/)

Allied subject associations are:

The Historical Association (www.history.org.uk/)

The Schools History project (www.schoolshistoryproject.co.uk/)

North American subject associations:

American Classical League (www.aclclassics.org/)

Society for Classical Studies (https://classicalstudies.org/)

## Conferences and events

The Classical Association conference (https://classicalassociation.org/events.html)

ARLT Refresher Day and Summer School, run by teachers for teachers (www.arlt.co.uk/)

Cambridge School Classics Project Conference (www.cambridgescp.com)

Hands Up Education conference (https://hands-up-education.org/conference24.html)

British Museum events (www.britishmuseum.org/learn/schools/ages-16)

Other events are organised by Classics for All, Advocating Classics Education or individual universities. Follow key individuals on social media for latest updates.

## Additional websites

Advocating Classics Education (https://aceclassics.org.uk/)

Asterion: Celebrating Neurodiversity in Classics (https://asterion.uk/)

British Museum (www.britishmuseum.org/)

Classics for All book reviews (https://classicsforall.org.uk/reading-room)

Classics in Communities (www.classicsincommunities.org/)

Eduqas Latin page (www.eduqas.co.uk/qualifications/latin-gcse/#tab_keydocuments)

OCR Classics page, with links to all examination syllabuses and specifications (www.ocr.org.uk/subjects/classics/)

TES Jobs (www.tes.com/jobs/)

## X

One of the best ways to keep up to date on good practice in Classics education is to maintain an active digital profile on X. This will allow you to make connections with teachers and academics in Classics and to 'observe' classroom practice elsewhere. It is also an excellent way to build a network of colleagues for resource co-creation and sharing. A curated list of classicists to follow is here: https://twitter.com/i/lists/856023530726727680. You might start with @jessbisc, @profarlenehh, @edithmayhall, @stephenjenkin, @wmarybeard, @classicsforall, @classical_assoc @arltclassics

## Higher education

For a list of UK universities offering classical courses, see the Council of UK Classics departments: https://cucd.blogs.sas.ac.uk/

For a comparison of the entry requirements, and courses available, see Holmes-Henderson, A. and Watts, B. (2021).

# BIBLIOGRAPHY

Agarwal, P. K. and Bain, P. M. (2019) *Powerful Teaching: Unleash the Science of Learning*. John Wiley & Sons.

Allison, S. and Tharby, A. (2015) *Making Every Lesson Count: Six Principles to Support Great Teaching and Learning*. Crown Publishing House.

Almasi, J. F. and King Fullerton, S. (2012) *Teaching Strategic Processes in Reading*. Guilford Publications.

Andersen, I. G. and Andersen, S. C. (2017) 'Student-centered instruction and academic achievement: Linking mechanisms of educational inequality to schools' instructional strategy', *British Journal of Sociology of Education*, 38(4), pp. 533–550.

Ausubel, D. (1963) *The Psychology of Meaningful Verbal Learning*. Grune & Stratton.

Beard, M. (2016) *SPQR: A History of Ancient Rome*. Profile Books.

Beck, I., L., Kucan, L. and McKeown, M. G. (2013) *Bringing words to life: Robust vocabulary instruction*. 2nd edn. The Guilford Press.

Bloor, A., McCabe, M. and Holmes-Henderson, A. (2023) 'Using classical mythology to teach English as an Additional Language', in Holmes-Henderson, A. (ed.) *Expanding Classics*, Routledge.

Bourke, S. (2008) *The Middle East: The Cradle of Civilization Revealed*. Thames & Hudson.

British Council Northern Ireland (2019) *Language Trends Northern Ireland 2019: Findings from surveys of primary and post-primary schools*. https://nireland.britishcouncil.org/sites/default/files/language_trends_final_web_version.pdf

British Council Northern Ireland (2021) *Language Trends Northern Ireland 2021*. https://nireland.britishcouncil.org/sites/default/files/m003_01_language_trends_ni_report_final_web_v2.pdf

Bruner, J. (1960) *The Process of Education: Revised Edition*. Harvard.

Bulwer, J. (2006) *Classics Teaching in Europe*. Duckworth.

Burnett, C. and Coldwell, M. (2021) 'Randomised controlled trials and the interventionisation of education', *Oxford Review of Education*, 47(4), pp. 423–438.

CCEA (Council for the Curriculum, Examinations & Assessment) (2007) *Curriculum*. https://ccea.org.uk/about/what-we-do/curriculum

Chi, M. T. H., Feltovich, P. J. and Glaser, R. (1981) 'Categorization and representation of physics problems by experts and novices', *Cognitive Science*, 5(2), pp. 121–152.

Cowan, N. (2010) 'The magical mystery four: How is working memory capacity limited, and why?', *Current Directions in Psychological Science*, 19(1), pp. 51–57.

EEF (Education Endowment Foundation) (2021) 'Special Educational Needs in Mainstream Schools Guidance Report', https://d2tic4wvo1iusb.cloudfront.net/production/eef-guidance-reports/send/EEF_Special_Educational_Needs_in_Mainstream_Schools_Guidance_Report.pdf?v=1705222655

Enser, Z. and Enser, M. (2020) *Fiorella and Mayer's Generative Learning in Action*. John Catt.

Fiorella, L. and Mayer, R. E. (2015) *Learning as a Generative Activity: Eight Learning Strategies that Promote Understanding*. Cambridge University Press.

Fisher, L. (2001) 'Modern foreign languages recruitment post-16: The pupils' perspective', *Language Learning Journal*, 23, pp. 33–40.

Flipped Learning Network (2014) *The Four Pillars of F-L-I-P*. https://flippedlearning.org/wp-content/uploads/2016/07/FLIP_handout_FNL_Web.pdf

Foster, F. and Wise, J. (2022) 'Social tensions in studying Ancient History', *The Curriculum Journal*, 33(4), pp. 536–552.

Gagne, E. (1985) *The Cognitive Psychology of School Learning*. HarperCollins.

Gall, A. (2020) 'A study in the use of embedded readings to improve the accessibility and understanding of Latin literature at A Level', *Journal of Classics Teaching*, 21(41), pp. 12–18.

Grabe, W. and Yamashita, J. (2022) *Reading in a Second Language: Moving from Theory to Practice*. 2nd edn. Cambridge University Press.

Gruber-Miller, J. (2006) *When Dead Tongues Speak: Teaching Beginning Greek and Latin*. Oxford University Press.

Hamilton, R. (1991) 'Reading Latin', *The Classical Journal*, 87(2), pp. 165–174.

Hanink, J. (2021, February 11) 'If Classics doesn't change, let it burn', *The Chronicle of Higher Education*.

Hattie, J. and Timperley, H. (2007) 'The power of feedback', *Review of Educational Research*, 77(1), pp. 81–112.

Hattie, J. and Yates, G. C. R. (2013) *Visible Learning and the Science of How We Learn*. Taylor & Francis Group.

Holmes-Henderson, A. (2023a) 'Ancient languages for 6- to 11-year-olds: Exploring three pedagogical approaches via a longitudinal study', in Holmes-Henderson, A. (ed.) *Expanding Classics: Practitioner Perspectives from Museums and Schools*. Routledge.

Holmes-Henderson, A. (ed.) (2023b) *Expanding Classics: Practitioner Perspectives from Museums and Schools*. Routledge.

Holmes-Henderson, A., Hunt, S. and Musié, M. (eds.) (2018) *Forward with Classics: Classical Languages in Schools and Communities*. Bloomsbury Academic.

Holmes-Henderson, A. and Kelly, K. (2022) *Ancient languages in primary schools in England: A literature review*. Department for Education. https://assets.publishing.service.gov.uk/government/uploads/system/uploads/attachment_data/file/1120024/Ancient_languages_in_primary_schools_in_England_-_A_Literature_Review.pdf

Holmes-Henderson, A. and Kelly, K. (2023) 'Learn the root. Conquer the word. Investigating the efficacy of *Vocabulous* in teaching word roots', Christ Church Research Centre.

Holmes-Henderson, A. and Watts, B. (2021) 'What grades are needed to study Classical subjects at UK universities?', *Journal of Classics Teaching*, 22(44), pp. 86–92.

Hunt, S. (2022) *Teaching Latin: Contexts, Theories and Practice*. Bloomsbury.

Hunt, S. (2023) *Starting to Teach Latin*. 2nd edn. Bloomsbury.

Hunt, S. and Holmes-Henderson, A. (2021) 'A level Classics poverty. Classical subjects in schools in England: Access, attainment and progression', *Council of University Classical Departments Bulletin*, 50, pp. 1–26. https://cucd.blogs.sas.ac.uk/files/2021/02/Holmes-Henderson-and-Hunt-Classics-Poverty.docx.pdf

Huxham, M. (2007) 'Fast and effective feedback: Are model answers the answer?', *Assessment & Evaluation in Higher Education*, 32(6), pp. 601–611.

Jones, K. (2019) *Retrieval Practice: Research and Resources for Every Classroom*. John Catt.

Kalyuga, S. (2007) 'Expertise reversal effect and its implications for learner-tailored instruction', *Educational Psychology Review*, 19(4), pp. 509–539.

Kalyuga, S., Ayres, P. L., Chandler, P. A. and Sweller, J. (2003) 'The expertise reversal effect', *Educational Psychologist*, 38(1), pp. 23–31.

Karpicke, J. D. and Roediger, H. L. (2008) 'The critical importance of retrieval for learning', *Science*, 319(5865), pp. 966–968.

Kirschner, P. A., Sweller, J. and Clark, R. E. (2006) 'Why minimal guidance during instruction does not work: An analysis of the failure of constructivist, discovery, problem-based, experiential, and inquiry-based teaching', *Educational Psychologist*, 41(2), pp. 75–86.

Li, J., Zhang, E.-H., Zhang, H., Gou, H. and Cao, H.-W. (2024) 'Retrieval practice plus feedback benefits a third language vocabulary learning', *International Journal of Multilingualism*, 21(2), pp. 1014–1033.

Lister, R. (2007) *Changing Classics in Schools*. Cambridge University Press.

Lloyd, M. and Hunt, S. (2020) *Communicative Approaches for Ancient Languages*. Bloomsbury Academic.

Lovell, O. (2020) *Sweller's Cognitive Load Theory in Action*. John Catt.

Lucas, E. (2021) 'Gaining understanding of different perspectives in Virgil's *Aeneid* through creative writing: An action research project with a sixth form Classical Civilisation class in a mixed comprehensive', *Journal of Classics Teaching*, 22(43), pp. 29–37.

Markus, D. D. and Ross, D. P. (2004) 'Reading proficiency in Latin through expectations and visualization', *The Classical World*, 98(1), pp. 79–93.

McCaffrey, D. V. (2009) 'When reading Latin, read as the Romans did', *The Classical Outlook*, 86(2), pp. 62–66.

McOmish, A. (2023) 'Promoting inclusivity through teaching Ancient History', in Holmes-Henderson, A. (ed.) *Expanding Classics: Practitioner Perspectives from Museums and Schools*. Routledge.

Mills, S. (2006) *Euripides. Bacchae*. Duckworth.

Mokhtari, K. and Reichard, C. A. (2002) 'Assessing students' metacognitive awareness of reading strategies', *Journal of Educational Psychology*, 94(2), pp. 249–259.

Morwood, J. (2003) *The Teaching of Classics*. Cambridge University Press.

Natoli, B. and Hunt, S. (eds.) (2019) *Teaching Classics with Technology*. Bloomsbury Academic.

Nuthall, G. (2007) *The Hidden Lives of Learners* NZCER Press.

Olivey, J. (2022, April 6) 'Creating a progression model for teaching historical perspectives in Key Stage 3', The Historical Association. www.history.org.uk/publications/resource/10401/creating-a-progression-model-for-teaching-historic

Perry, J., Lundie, D. and Golder, G. (2019) 'Metacognition in schools: What does the literature suggest about the effectiveness of teaching metacognition in schools?' *Educational Review*, 71(4), pp. 483–500.

Poser, R. (2021, February 2) 'He wants to save Classics from whiteness. Can the field survive?', *The New York Times*. www.nytimes.com/2021/02/02/magazine/classics-greece-rome-whiteness.html

Praet, S. and Verhelst, B. (2020) 'Teaching translation theory and practice', *Journal of Classics Teaching*, 21(42), pp. 31–35.

Quigley, A. (2018) *Closing the Vocabulary Gap*. Taylor & Francis Group.

Roediger, H. L. and Karpicke, J. D. (2006). 'Test-enhanced learning: Taking memory tests improves long-term retention', *Psychological Science*, 17(3), pp. 249–255.

Rosenshine, B. (2012) 'Principles of instruction: Research-based strategies that all teachers should know', *The Education Digest*, 78(3), pp. 30–40.

Russell, K. (2018) 'Read like a Roman: Teaching students to read in Latin word order', *Journal of Classics Teaching*, 19(37), pp. 17–29.

Ryan, R. M. and Deci, E. L. (2020) 'Intrinsic and extrinsic motivation from a self-determination theory perspective: Definitions, theory, practices, and future directions', *Contemporary Educational Psychology*, 61, 101860.

Schunk, D. H. (1981) 'Modeling and attributional effects on children's achievement: A self-efficacy analysis', *Journal of Educational Psychology*, 73(1), pp. 93–105.

Scott, J. A. and Nagy, W. E. (1997) 'Understanding the definitions of unfamiliar verbs', *Reading Research Quarterly*, 32(2), pp. 184–200.

Sears, L. L. and Ballestrini, K. (2019) 'Adapting antiquity: Using tiered texts to increase Latin reading proficiency', *Journal of Classics Teaching*, 20(39), pp. 71–77.

Sherrington, T. (2017) *The Learning Rainforest: Great Teaching in Real Classrooms*. John Catt.

Sherrington, T. (2019) *Rosenshine's Principles in Action*. John Catt.

Swalec, J. (2023) 'Visual translation: A creative tool for practising metacognition and analysing agency and power', *Journal of Classics Teaching*, 24(47), pp. 12–15.

Swallow, P. (2023) 'Teaching difficult stories: Trauma-informed teaching in the Classics classroom', *Journal of Classics Teaching*, 24(48), pp. 162–164.

Sykes, R. (2021) 'Can studying a topic through a reception approach improve the quality of Year 7 students' creative responses to the ancient world?', *Journal of Classics Teaching*, 22(43), pp. 4–21.

Taylor, A., Holmes-Henderson, A. and Jones, S. (2023) 'Classics education in Northern Irish primary schools; curriculum policy and classroom practice', *Journal of Classics Teaching*, 24(47), pp. 52–58.

Taylor, G., Jungert, T., Mageau, G. A., Schattke, K., Dedic, H., Rosenfield, S. and Koestner, R. (2014) 'A self-determination theory approach to predicting school achievement over time: The unique role of intrinsic motivation', *Contemporary Educational Psychology*, 39(4), pp. 342–358.

Teng, F. (2022) 'The benefits of metacognitive reading strategy awareness instruction for young learners of English as a second language', *Literacy*, 54(1), pp. 29–39.

Umachandran, M. and Ward, M. (eds.) (2023) *Critical Ancient World Studies: The Case for Forgetting Classics.* Routledge.

van Gog, T., Rummel, N. and Renkl, A. (2019) 'Learning how to solve problems by studying examples', in Dunlosky, J. and Rawson, K. A. (eds.) *The Cambridge Handbook of Cognition and Education*, pp. 183–208. Cambridge University Press.

Wang, M. C., Haertel, G. D. and Walberg, H. J. (1990) 'What influences learning? A content analysis of review literature', *Journal of Educational Research*, 84(1), pp. 30–38.

Welsh Government (2023) *Curriculum for Wales: Annual Report 2023.* www.gov.wales/curriculum-wales-annual-report-2023-html

Whittaker, P. and Hayes, R. (2018) *Essential Tips for the Inclusive Secondary Classroom: A Road Map to Quality-First Teaching.* 1st edn. Routledge.

Wiliam, D. (2017) *Embedded Formative Assessment: Strategies for Classroom Assessment That Drives Student Engagement and Learning.* Solution Tree.

Williams, R. D. (2009) *The Aeneid.* Bristol Classical Press.

Wilson, E. (2017) *The Odyssey.* W. W. Norton & Company.

Woolcock, N. (2023, June 29) 'Latin is now fourth most-taught language in primary schools', www.thetimes.co.uk/article/latin-language-lessons-uk-primary-schools-2023-wrqrtfj0s

Woolcock, N. (2024, April 26) '"Expelliarmus!" The primary schools ditching French for Latin', www.thetimes.co.uk/article/the-primary-schools-ditching-french-for-latin-ck6g60kx2

Wright, P. (2023) 'Including the excluded: Teaching Latin in an area of high socio-economic disadvantage', in Holmes-Henderson, A. (ed.) *Expanding Classics: Practitioner Perspectives from Museums and Schools*. Routledge.

Yang, C., Luo, L., Vadillo, M. A., Yu, R. and Shanks, D. R. (2021) 'Testing (quizzing) boosts classroom learning: A systematic and meta-analytic review', *Psychological Bulletin*, 147(4), pp. 399–435.

Zimmerman, B. J. (1989) 'A social cognitive view of self-regulated academic learning', *Journal of Educational Psychology*, 81(3), pp. 329–339.

Zuckerberg, D. (2019, April) 'Burn it all down?'. Eidolon. https://eidolon.pub/burn-it-all-down-182f5edb16e